AMPLIFY

YOUR

VALUE

Leading IT with Strategic Vision

JEFFREY S TON

ALSO BY JEFFREY S. TON

BLOGS

Rivers of Thought -
https://riversofthought.net/

People Development Magazine -
https://peopledevelopmentmagazine.com/author/jeff-ton/

Intel IT Peer Network -
https://itpeernetwork.intel.com/author/jtongici/#

Institute for Digital Transformation -
https://www.institutefordigitaltransformation.org/
digital-era-now/

Forbes Technology Council -
https://www.forbes.com/sites/forbestechcouncil/people/
jeffreyton/

What others have said...

"The CIO's role has never been more strategic. But succeeding in today's agile and speed-is-value market demands more than the IT strategies of the past — it requires a strategic vision that will help you guide your organization during an exciting, but tumultuous journey to the future. This book is your playbook for creating and executing just this sort of vision from a CIO who's done it — and has the accolades and battle scars to prove it. If you're a CIO or senior IT leader, consider it required reading."

— Charles Araujo, Industry Analyst, Founder of The Institute for Digital Transformation, and Author of *The Quantum Age of IT: Why Everything You Know About IT is About to Change*

"As a seasoned technology leader, Jeff shares his majestic career journey with authentic vulnerability. It is refreshing to see such a thoughtful and strategic perspective for technology leaders to learn from. The five business models framework maps tangible steps to take action right way!"

— Julie Kratz, Founder, CEO of Pivot Point, Author of *One*

"Jeff tells a compelling story of being a CIO in the trenches — taking charge when opportunities present themselves, shoring up operations when required, and evolving strategies that drive business results. IT leaders will relate to his challenges and learn best practices from an experienced leader."

— Isaac Sacolick, President and CIO of StarCIO and Author of *Driving Digital*

"Jeff's right. The CIO is best placed to lead strategically in the face of perpetual transformation. His own journey to a seat at the table won him many battle scars. He has used that experience to craft a must-read book for any CIO that wants to know how to lead IT with strategic vision from a seat at the executive table. It is a blueprint to shift from keeping the lights on to the kind of enterprise that not only avoids disruption but builds a strategic competence of innovation."

— **Ron J. West, CEO of West Executive Inc and creator of The Chrysalis Program**

Foreword by
Will Lasalle

AMPLIFY YOUR VALUE

*Leading IT with
Strategic Vision*

JEFFREY S TON

Cover Design: Venkata RamaRao.K, on 99Designs
Interior Design: 3Cs Books
Graphic Design: Jenny Kowalski
Amplify Dial Image: Copyright: Le Moal Olivier

Tradepaper ISBN: 978-0-692-11418-6
Digital ISBN: 978-0-692-11419-3

ACKNOWLEDGMENTS

Writing a book is like raising a child; it takes a village. For me, it has taken a good part of a career, a career of leading information technology departments and divisions. The accomplishments you will read of in *Amplify Your Value* would not have been possible without a multitude of people. I'd like to take a moment to thank many of them here.

I must start by acknowledging the many IT professionals I have had the privilege of working alongside. First, the team at Lauth Group: Aaron Booth, Michelle Ross Campbell, Barry Crump, Jeremiah Dominque, Teresa Donsbach, Alan Francouer, Bea Gustin, Beau Hainsworth, Jamal Handy, Mike Harris, Mike Harris, Jr., Derek Hartman, Kris Hayes, Joe Holtel, Tim Holtz, Steve Johnson, Jason Jones, Marcia Kalasmiki, Greg Melton, Norberto Monarrez, Paula Murray, Ryan Schroeder, Jarod Stone, Kris Stone, Carrie Tarver, Todd Werner, Mike Wilson.

The Team at Goodwill Industries of Central and Southern Indiana included: Jeff Allen, Brandon

Alexander, Debbie Babcock, Kayla Bennett, Joy Bosley, Ty Caldwell, Betsy Chambers, Li Chang, Julie Clark, Dennis Cuffel, Stanley Dixon, Andy Deubner, Chad Downey, Rodney Duke, Matt Durr, Jason Fisher, Dave Francis, Ben Frederick, Scott Gorrell, Kelvin Hart, Iain Henderson, Scot Johnson, Imran Khan, Patrick Leboehi, Muhammad Maaita, Tabitha Manross, Melissa McGinley, Greg McIntyre, Jeff Perrey, Ed Roze, Kurt Reusze, Sarah Stiver, Darren Touseull, Jeremy Vaughn, Matt Weber, Daniel Whitmyer.

Neither of these lists would be complete without Paula Isenhower and Kay Haimes, my right hand and left hands at Lauth and Goodwill, respectively!

In these pages, I tell the story of developing the breakthrough image for the Lauth IT strategic plan. Matt Cashatt deserves the credit for the idea and helping me to bring it to life. Matt, thank you!

Most of my tenure at Lauth, I had the privilege of working for Ron West. Much of who I am as a leader, I can trace back to those days. It wasn't always easy (for either of us), but growth never is.

At Goodwill, I had the privilege of working for and alongside two great leaders. Jim McClelland led the organization for over forty years. It was his belief that technology would be a strategic lever to enable the organization to grow and prosper that lead me to Goodwill in the first place. When Jim retired, Kent Kramer took over the reins. Prior to taking the CEO role, he was the Chief Operating Officer. The friendship and partnership he and I formed was the catalyst for many of the accomplishments you will read about here.

Throughout my career, I have been surrounded by an amazing set of mentors and colleagues. All have contributed in no small way to the thinking behind *Amplify Your Value*. All have earned a seat at the table, and all have led their organizations to achieve remarkable visions. Patrick Bogan, Jeff Dodson, Ginny Davis, Gail Farnsley, John Frank, Aleta Jeffress, Glenn Keller, Tracy Kemp, Will Lasalle, Isaac Sacolick, David Schacht, Teresa Conroy-Roth, Judd Williams, Pete Williams...thank you! Thank you for sharing your insights, thank you for driving me to be better, thank you for being friends as well as colleagues.

Finally, Dr. Dan Miller of Historical Solutions has been my executive coach for well over five years. Dan, it has been an amazing river! I look forward to the bends ahead!

FOREWORD

Jeff Ton's book, *Amplify Your Value,* is being published at a time where the role of IT-focused executives such as Chief Information Officers, Chief Technology Officers, Chief Information Security Officers and Chief Digital Officers and their departments are under more scrutiny than ever before. Jeff's tales and strategies demonstrate how IT can not only amplify its value to the organization but also how an IT executive can amplify his/her own career value.

Jeff speaks to IT leaders in a manner that is not only easy to understand but encourages them to think differently. The stories in the book demonstrate that EQ (Emotional Quotient) is just as important if not more important than IQ (Intelligence Quotient) when it comes to demonstrating IT's value in the current business landscape.

I've known Jeff for several years and have always respected his knowledge and insight. So much so that even as one of the most influential and social Information Technology & Security Officers in the world, when I was looking to expand JLS Technology USA's service offerings, I spoke with Jeff at length, explaining the idea and strategic plan while soliciting his feedback. His thoughts and perspective helped me immensely in being able to successfully execute and deliver for our client base.

I believe in lifelong learning and continual improvement. I was able to incorporate some of Jeff's teachings and approaches into my client base to great success and reception.

As I read through *Amplify Your Value*, I couldn't help but feel the same way I do when I speak with Jeff during one of our strategy and catch-up calls: feelings of profound insight, excitement and motivation! You will feel the same way, too. Cheesy technology humor included!

Will Lassalle
Chief Information Officer
JLS Technology USA

DEDICATION

To my co-Captain in life, my wife, my muse,
my best friend, Carmen.

Without whom I would not have found my voice!

TABLE OF CONTENTS

INTRODUCTION

What is holding you back from leading with a strategic vision?

When I posed that question to a room full of CIOs and senior IT leaders, the answers were varied:

> "I don't feel like we [IT] are aligned with the business."

> "They [the business] don't see the value in IT and what we can do."

> "We spend 80 to 85 percent of our time keeping the lights on. Who has time for strategy and vision?"

> "I don't know where to start."

It seems like many IT leaders have been fighting to get a seat at the proverbial table since the title of Chief Information Officer was first created in the early 1980s.

Yet I struggle to name a business today that does not rely on information technology to operate. Take away the applications, take away the systems, and it would be like disconnecting the power from the building. What do companies do when faced with an extended power outage? They send everyone home.

In this age of digital transformation and digital disruption, information technology is moving center stage, from the backroom to the boardroom. The proliferation of CxO titles like CTO, CDO, CSO, etc., is a sign many companies realize they need help. They need someone to navigate; they need strategy; they need vision, and they need someone to lead with a strategic vision.

Enter the CIO (or VP of IT, or Director of IT). Who better to lead this charge than the person who has his or her finger on the pulse of every aspect of the business? The CIO is in a unique position in most organizations. She is involved in almost every initiative in the company. She sees the challenges faced by one line of business and see attempts by other lines to solve comparable challenges. She is uniquely qualified to address these challenges and lead their businesses forward.

Whether you are a seasoned CIO, new to the role, or aspire to achieve that office, you can and must lead this charge. Don't know where to start? Then this book is for you! Throughout these pages, I will show you a process you can use to transform your department. You can swing the pendulum of keeping the lights on toward innovation; you can increase your agility and elasticity (and that of the business). You *can* earn a seat at the table. And you can lead with a strategic vision.

I've been there. I've earned the battle scars. I've made it to the table, and you can too!

OK, so who *is* this guy?

I started my career in IT at about the same time the title of CIO was created in the early 80s. My first real job in IT was in the information systems department for a large local bank. Before transferring to IS, I worked in the end-user reporting department for their credit card division. My big break came when I got the job of "Remote Data Center Manager." Sounds fancy, I know. What it really meant was I had the responsibility for distributing the green-bar printouts to a team of 200 or so programmers in an office building down the street from the bank's headquarters. (Don't know what green-bar is? Computers used to print on continuous reams of paper, fed through the dot matrix printers by perforated strips on either side. The paper was shaded with alternating bars of green to make the text more readable. Still confused? Ask a geezer!)

From that auspicious start, I worked my way up through the ranks of programmers: Programmer Analyst I, II and III. In 1989, a friend and I started a business whose mission was to build custom xBase applications for small businesses. What started as two guys in a back-room grew into a company with a handful of employees and mid-six-digit gross revenue. For a variety of reasons, not the least of which was the need for a consistent paycheck, we sold the business in 1992, and I went to work as a hired gun for a local IT consulting firm, Software Synergy, Inc. (now Theoris).

I worked as a contract developer and team lead at Thomson Multimedia (now Technicolor) for six years and another eight as an employee. During those years, I made the jump into management. By the time my tenure at Thomson was ending, I was the director of the shared services organization with teams on four different continents, a couple of hundred outsourced developers in India, and enough airline miles that it would take the next five years to use them all.

In early 2006, I was at a crossroads. I could stay with Thomson. However, to do so would mean taking a temporary expat assignment in Paris or a relocation to southern California. My wife, Carmen, and I seriously considered the expat option. We loved Paris. In the end, we decided we didn't want to leave Central Indiana. I felt ready for the next stage in my IT career: CIO. By spring of that year, I was the Vice President of Enterprise Process & Information Technology at Lauth Group, a billion-dollar commercial real estate developer.

At Lauth, I tried my hand at transforming the department into an equal partner with the rest of the business, giving it the ability to support the company's meteoric growth. Throughout this book, I will discuss many of the lessons learned through this time—what worked and what didn't. That experience laid the foundation for what was to be an amazing five-year journey, but I am getting ahead of myself.

You may recall 2008 was not kind to commercial real estate. It was especially rough for firms like Lauth, whose primary revenue source was new development. No one was investing in new real estate development. After two or three rounds of layoffs to "right size" the organization, I approached the partners to discuss putting my name on the list for the next round. "I'm a strategic CIO. With the size we are becoming, you are going to need someone who can fix your PCs, and that's not me." With that, I launched my second small business.

I spent the next year trying to build a green business consultancy, of all things. Always a tree-hugger, I had learned about green building techniques while at Lauth. Besides, I had had enough of this IT thing. I had poured my heart and soul into building an amazing team, only to dismantle it in six short months. I was devastated. I was tired. I was done.

Confluence Dynamics (I still think that is the coolest name for a company, taken from the concepts of the fluid dynamics at work at the confluence of two rivers) never really caught on. Again, the lessons learned could fill a book, but as 2009 was coming to a close, I knew I needed to return to what I knew best, what I loved the most, and what I was good at: IT. As I launched my job search, I began to do some IT management consulting gigs for Resources Global Professionals. Through those gigs, I was able to build upon the framework I had started at Lauth, one that provides a great 360-degree view of an IT department (more on that in the first chapter).

Within a few short months, I became the Chief Information Officer for Goodwill Industries of Central Indiana. It was a dream job and a perfect fit. You could lay my resume side by side with the job description and they'd line up perfectly. In May of 2010, we began an amazing journey. Looking back on those five years, I am proud of everything we accomplished. It is those five years that form the basis of much of this book. However, that journey would not have been possible without the blood, sweat, and tears that came before it.

The journey took just shy of five years. We succeeded in taking an 80-year-old organization and migrating its architecture to one that is 100 percent cloud-based. (OK, the purists out there will dispute my math of 100 percent and perhaps even my definition of cloud but stick with me).

2014 (plus the first 10 days of 2015) saw the completion of the three final steps on this journey. The year started with the implementation of Recovery as a Service (RaaS), modernizing the disaster recovery processes and providing a Recovery Time Objective (RTO) of under two hours and a Recovery Point Objective (RPO) of—get this—THIRTY SECONDS! (Insert legal disclaimer here: "our experience may not match your actual results; SLAs do apply.") Too good to be true? We've done it.

The next step was the migration of the headend of the network to a Tier IV data center on the east side of town. We have had a hub and spoke network topology for many years. However, the hub was the headquarters building. Far from a Tier IV data center, we had a server room (read: glorified closet), no raised floor, cooling provided by a single Lieber unit, water-based fire suppression (OK, we fixed THAT years ago), and no backup power supply. Now, the headquarters building is just another 70+ spokes on the network.

The final step we took on January 10 was the migration of all the production and test servers and data storage arrays into a virtual private cloud hosted by Bluelock (now Bluelock Solutions from InterVision), an Indianapolis-based cloud company. The task was incredibly complex. Imagine taking apart your car, shipping the pieces to another location, then putting it back together again, AND have it all work when you are done, AND not disrupting your family's transportation needs during the move. That is basically what the team accomplished. They moved 75 servers, over 200 applications, several thousand device addresses and 15 terabytes of data, all on a Saturday night.

What did our company gain from these efforts? In short, agility and elasticity. First agility: any new project going forward will no longer require the lead time to order a server, configure the server and deploy the server. This step now takes minutes—talk about agile! We no longer have to replace the servers every three or four years, spending capital and months of IT time to plan, order, and execute an upgrade. We no longer have to upgrade the server operating systems or our middleware software. That frees our staff to work on projects that provide more value to Goodwill, like the call tree for retail Home Pick Up, the mobile devices for nursing, or our data architecture project that will provide improved reporting, data analytics, and insights.

Next, we gained elasticity, which means as we continue to grow we do not have to stair-step the infrastructure to keep pace—buying more capacity than we need to ensure the capacity is there when we need it. This is the typical approach to infrastructure because the lead time to deploy capacity is so long. Now, for Goodwill, it is moments. Conversely, if we ever had to shrink our infrastructure footprint, it would only take a phone call—no contract negotiations, no selling off assets, just a phone call.

The position of Goodwill Industries of Central & Southern Indiana today is unique among most other non-profits and the majority of for-profit companies. They are on target for a fantastic future, which is an amazing accomplishment by an amazing team of IT professionals. In my more than three decades of IT work, I have never seen anything like it. I have seen data center moves that took days or weeks to complete (and the business was down during those times). I have seen at least one case where the entire move was canceled because it was deemed too costly and risky.

Throughout this book, we will explore the steps the teams at Lauth and Goodwill took to mature the departments, grow as IT professionals, and amplify their value within their businesses.

Ready? Let's get started!

In the chapters ahead, I will map the steps you need to take to align your department with your business. IT's value will be apparent for all to see. You will be able to swing the pendulum away from "keeping the lights on" toward innovation. You will learn how to define a strategy that looks two, three, even five years down the road. In short, this book will show you how to amplify your value and lead IT with strategic vision by transforming your IT department into a lean, mean fighting machine!

BUILDING
THE
STRATEGY

LET'S GET ALIGNED

What does it mean to lead IT with a strategic vision? At its core, it means always leading with your mind on your destination. Everything you do, every decision you make, even the detours you take, get you closer to that destination. Leading with strategic vision means you develop and implement programs that enable you to reach your destination.

Many books have been written and many consultants have made a fine living helping companies develop their vision statements. But a vision is more than just a statement. Your vision should paint a picture. It will answer the question "Why does your company (or department, or team, or even your career) exist and what will it look like three years from now?" The vision statement will be your rallying cry. It should conjure up in the minds of those who hear it exactly what you hope for and care about as a company (or team or individual).

Let's use a simple example. When I say the word "ball," what image pops into your head? It might be a basketball, a baseball, a soccer ball or one of a hundred different kinds of ball. But what if I say baseball? Even then, some may picture an old tattered ball they used to play with as a kid, while others may imagine a brand-new ball just out of the wrapper. Some may think of the autographed ball sitting on a shelf in their office, and some may even think of the rubberized ball they use to play catch with their young child.

Now imagine that as a team, we spent time describing and agreeing upon—painting a picture on our mental canvas—our image of a baseball: a pristine white ball, just out of the wrapper. Imagine we discussed the softness of the leather; the red stitching feeling like a miniature washboard, a stark contrast to the white of the leather; the Rawlings logo; the MLB logo with the "Official Major League Baseball" trademark, and the signature of Commissioner Rob Manfred. Had we spent this time, chances are the phrase, "IT, Let's Play Ball!" would conjure up the same image to all of us.

That is the type of detailed image your strategic vision should bring to mind. This vision will undoubtedly be different than the overall corporate vision statement, but it should support it. In other words, if IT achieves its vision, the company will have achieved its vision (or at least be significantly closer to achieving it).

To achieve this vision, you will need strategies. These are your "hows." How will you travel the journey towards your goal? In some ways, this can be even more difficult than painting the picture of your vision. As IT professionals, we tend to go straight to the "what." We are going to execute this project or that project; we are going to implement these processes, or we are going to replace the core application. While these may all be important, they don't answer the how.

Throughout this book, we will explore various strategies that were developed through the course of creating strategic plans for different organizations. These strategies included a cloud strategy, how and when we would leverage cloud; an A-C/C-F strategy, how and when we would self-perform work and how and when we would use partners; a core principles strategy, how we would behave, make decisions, invoke the Governance Team; and several others.

This book is for the CIO, Vice President of IT, Director of IT, or whatever your title may be. You are the highest-ranking IT professional in your organization. You may be new to the role of CIO, be a veteran IT leader starting at a new organization, or you may have been in your role for quite some time and are looking for new ways to guide your department.

If you are not the top IT person in your company, don't put this book down just yet. You may be leading a team within a larger IT department, or you may aspire to be the CIO. You will learn valuable skills throughout these pages that can help propel you to that destination.

If you have the desire (or your company is asking you) to go beyond managing the blinking lights, to drive your business forward, to be a leader within your organization, then this book is for you.

The strategies and the journeys described in this book will lead you to success. In the chapter "To Get Where You are Going," we explore the first step on the journey: the IT Assessment. If you have been in your role for longer than a year, I strongly suggest you leverage a third party to perform this assessment for you. While you and your team are probably quite capable of performing it, you will want the unbiased view a third party will bring.

The role of the CIO has evolved since the day the title was introduced. Today's CIO is called upon to be more than the guardian of the server room or data center. Today's CIO knows IT is more than a cost center. Technology is an integral part of every business in operation. Want to see its penetration? Take down the corporate network for an hour or two (no, I am not advocating you actually do this!) and see what happens: everyone goes home, unable to work.

The person who wants to lead IT with strategic vision must aspire to be more of a business person than a technologist. I won't say the days of an IT professional moving from industry to industry are past, but it is getting harder and harder. For the CIO who lives and breathes their business, the industry gets ingrained in who they are and how they think about technology.

What You Will Learn in this Book

This book is divided into two main sections: Building the Plan and Executing the Plan. In the remainder of the first section, we will discuss the steps you will need to take (including getting aligned) to develop an Information Technology Strategic Plan for your company.

- Assessing Current State – creating a 360-degree view of the department, including the context in which it operates

- Creating the Vision – developing a vision for the future is a pivotal step in your evolution

- Communication Techniques – seeking ways to obtain buy-in from all the constituents of the plan

- Understanding Architecture – looking beyond IT architecture to reveal your company's architecture

- Writing the Plan – the nuts and bolts of what to include in your plan, including some sample frameworks

- Improving Process – implementing processes that will set the foundation for success, even before you have finished writing the plan

Once the strategic plan is written, the vision adopted, and the stakeholders on board, it's time to put the binder on the shelf and go about your daily tasks of managing the blinking lights… NO! Now is the time to execute the plan! Now the work begins! In the section "Executing the Plan," we will offer some real examples and valuable lessons learned to help you ensure the success of your plan.

- Avoiding C-F Projects – identifying the projects that drive business value and how to stop doing those that don't

- Evergreen planning – strategies for ensuring the plan remains relevant and can be adjusted with changes in the business or technology

- Using the Core Principles – how the core principles are used to manage the day to day and how to use them to guide longer-term decisions

- Leveraging a Cloud Strategy – developing and using a cloud strategy to unleash the power in other parts of your plan

Now that we are aligned on what a strategic vision is, are you ready to lead with that vision? Are you ready to earn your seat at the table? Let's begin by building your vision and your plan.

2

TO GET WHERE YOU ARE GOING

To get where you are going, you have to know where you are. Sounds pretty obvious, doesn't it? To arrive at any destination, you have to leave where you are and move toward that destination. At the very least, you have to know where your starting point is in relation to your ending point.

Our journey to transform IT actually started during my interview process for the CIO role at Goodwill Industries of Central Indiana. As a candidate for the role, one of the steps was a meeting with the entire team. They would help choose the person they wanted to lead them.

17

WOW! Talk about intimidating, walking into a room of people who all have your resume in front of them. You've never met them; you don't even know their names, and *they* are helping to decide your future.

My host dropped me off at the conference room and left. Within moments of entering the room, I realized the team members were nervous, possibly even more nervous than I was. No one said a word. They were all looking at me. So, I just jumped right in. I kicked things off by introducing myself and then having them introduce themselves. I then asked for questions. Two questions in particular stood out.

"I see from your resume that you have worked for XYZ Company. I know they use Oracle. Are you going to replace Microsoft with Oracle?"

Interesting question. My answer? I couldn't possibly make any recommendation or decision of that magnitude with the information I have today. I would spend the first several weeks and months learning, listening, asking questions. If any change in technology seemed appropriate, it would be because we as a team decided it made sense.

"I see from your resume that you have done a lot of outsourcing. Are you going to outsource us?"

Another interesting question. My answer? Similar to the first. I couldn't possibly make any recommendation or decision...

This time, however, I answered more fully. I explained each of the outsourcing projects that I had been involved with in prior roles. I explained the business reasons for each, the benefits achieved, and the issues we experienced. Every business is different; every company is different. I cannot sit here in front of you today and say we would or we would not outsource any of our functions, but I will say, we will come to those conclusions (whatever those conclusions are) together.

Of course, by now, you realize I got the job! But, at the time, I could only imagine that going from this grilling to the interview with the CEO would be as intense as a Tony Robbins firewalk over hot coals!

The Assessment

As the new CIO, I wanted to get the lay of the land, to understand fully and deeply where we were and what we had. I had been a part of numerous IT assessments over my career, each one, it seems, using a different framework and methodology. During my career, I had taken what I felt were the best pieces of each and developed a process to get a picture of how an IT team was performing. I had used this process successfully at several companies, and now, I was going to use it on my own department.

After getting settled in for a couple of weeks, we kicked off an IT assessment. This assessment was an evaluation of Goodwill's current application architecture, infrastructure, staffing levels and skill sets. During this time, we reviewed system documentation, attended various staff and project meetings, interviewed key IT resources, participated in issue resolution, and analyzed application configurations.

The purpose was to review the company's information technology assets and deliver an executive-level report, detailing and summarizing our evaluation of risk associated with the current IT environment, platforms, and required level of support.

The approach during the assessment focused on the following characteristics:

1. Scalability – how the current environment would handle double the volume or more

2. Maintainability – how much duplicate effort is spent supporting the current environment

3. Reliability – how well the current environment performs

4. Supportability – what organizational skills or investments in end-user training/tools are needed

5. Controllability – how secure is the environment

You may be thinking, "I thought we were talking about strategic vision here. These are pretty traditional characteristics." And you'd be right. These are table stakes. If you want a seat at the table, if you're going to lead with strategic vision, you *must* be doing these things well.

Scalability, maintainability, reliability, supportability, and controllability are the foundation of a stable technology platform. Gaps in any one of these will limit your credibility throughout your organization. It will be difficult to have strategic conversations with the heads of the business units if the IT systems are not stable, for example. Every conversation will devolve to a discussion about up-time (or the lack thereof). If you are trying to break out of the "order taker" persona, it will be impossible if your help desk is not easy to work with. If every conversation involving new business ideas ends with you saying "No," it will build the wrong reputation for your department.

I have to pause here and talk about "no" for a minute. Many IT departments earn the reputation of being the department that says no. Yet most never utter the word. What's going on here? It's in our approach. If we are always talking about risks, or why something won't work, or how busy we are, what our business partners hear is "no." All of those things may be true, but we have to change the conversation from why it won't work to how it could work. More on the language of IT in a later chapter. For now, let's get back to the assessment.

If you are managing IT and your assessment shows you scoring high marks in these areas, you and your team are a step ahead of most departments. More than likely, your assessment will reveal gaps that you must address. As you will see in later chapters, these gaps may be so significant you need to attack them even while you are building your plan.

The current state assessment that we performed at Goodwill was based on the principles of Control Objects for Information and related Technology (COBIT), Information Technology Infrastructure Library (ITIL) and Capability Maturity Model Integration (CMMI). It did not, however, represent a full audit under any of these frameworks. Using both my experience with these frameworks and my knowledge of the organization, I selected the controls from each that I thought would provide the clearest picture of our maturity and that, when implemented, would provide the most "bang for the buck." Candidly, I also didn't want to scare anyone by suggesting we needed hundreds of controls.

In addition, the current technical architecture was reviewed, and areas of risk, potential bottlenecks, and deviations from best practices were identified. As the risks were identified, the estimated probability of the risk occurring and the impact an occurrence would have on the organization were identified.

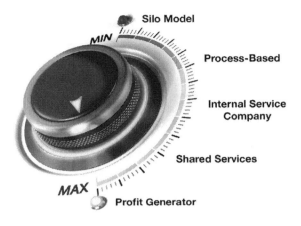

IT Business Models

During the assessment, we used the "Business Model Continuum" from Gartner. While Gartner's original used a horizontal axis, I view it as a dial—a dial to amplify your value. By cranking up the "volume" (value), you change your relationship with others in your business, and you change the way IT is viewed.

The dial breaks IT departments into five different business models:

- Silo Model is a department that is very reactive, viewed as a utility and treated with uncertainty. These departments have difficulty planning, typically do not adhere to schedules and have very little documentation.

- Process-Based Model has begun to implement some repeatable processes. This adds some predictability to the services they provide. They are able to be more proactive, even though they are still viewed with skepticism.

- Internal Service Company Model has matured into an organization that proactively manages its assets and works with the business to enhance the systems, thereby providing more value. They have a list of services they provide and act like a company within a company. This department is an accepted partner within the business.

- Shared Services Model takes the ISC model a step further and provides additional services to the organization by centralizing some of the operation and maintenance of the applications themselves. Typically, this is found in large multinational organizations with disparate business products.

- Profit Generator Model truly becomes part of the product. They are creating new ideas for generating revenue and are embedded in the process of design of new or enhanced product offerings. Very few departments ever reach this stage.

In understanding these models and using them to transform an IT department, there are two fundamental principles that must be adhered to. First, you can only crank up the volume as high as the culture of your business wants you to go. Your department cannot operate under the profit generator model, for example, if the company culture doesn't want you operating in that way.

If your head is bruised from beating it against a wall, you've probably advanced as far as you can around the dial. If this happens, and you believe strongly enough in what technology can do for your organization, you will need to begin to drive a culture change. This change starts at the top.

This mismatch of goals can manifest in a variety of different ways. Most often I've seen it in denied proposals. If, for example, you and your team have an idea for a new revenue stream for your company by leveraging its digital assets in some way, and you are not able to convince the other leaders in the business, look first at how you are communicating your idea. If you continue to hear no, review the dial. What stage are you in? Are you trying to go beyond the culture of the business?

The second principle is, as you turn the dial, you cannot skip a model. For example, you cannot move to the Internal Service Provider business model without first becoming process-based.

Because these models build upon themselves, each one laying the foundation for the next, skipping models can have disastrous results that the *next* CIO will have to fix. If you are trying to roll out a service catalogue as a part of your evolution to internal service provider and you don't have the underlying processes defined and implemented, your internal customers will revolt. Your service levels (you have defined service levels, right? You can't be a service provider without them) will never be met. Your customers will do an end run around your processes.

If you experience this, look first to your processes. Are they well defined? Are they repeatable? Are they followed consistently? Each click along the dial builds on the previous one. Each comes with new requirements that cannot be met without first excelling at the prior.

It Starts with the Business

One of the things that had attracted me to this position was Goodwill's desire to have their IT team be "more strategic." They knew that technology was a vital part of what they do to deliver their mission. They also knew that in order to continue to grow the business they would need an IT department that was fully aligned with the business goals and one that "thought strategically."

To perform an assessment of this nature you have to start at the beginning, with the business context in which the IT department operates. We conducted a series of meetings and interviews with the heads of each of the four business units and their direct reports. In addition, the heads of each of the support departments (of which IT was one) were also interviewed. The picture that began to emerge was of four disparate business units: Retail, Manufacturing, Education, and Mission, supported centrally by IT, Marketing, HR, and Finance, with the Foundation (the fundraising arm) off to the side.

The other major theme that came up was that the business leaders were hungry for IT to lead, to bring them ideas of how technology could further their businesses or their department. They were disappointed with the current level of support. They wanted much more.

A Look in the Mirror

The next step in the process was to turn our focus internally to the IT department itself. We reviewed each of the applications to understand its type (commercial, home-grown), its current release level, how well it was meeting the business's needs (admittedly, this was somewhat subjective) and how many support tickets were being generated.

The organization had just moved from a "best of breed" to an ERP shop. Thirty days after my arrival was the go-live of an ERP system, with Corporate and

Manufacturing being the first two areas converted. The roadmap called for Retail to be next. In fact, we were already in the pre-beta program with the vendor.

This also put us squarely in the "buy" versus "build" category. The department did have a development team that handled building point solutions to fill the gaps in the ERP, as well as extending and customizing the Retail Point of Sale. In fact, the POS had been so heavily customized that getting support from the vendor was impossible. And, upgrades? Fuhgeddaboudit!

We turned our attention to the infrastructure. Here, we looked at the age of the equipment, the patch levels of the operating systems, the warranty, the health of the network, and, of course, the number of support tickets generated. The team had recently completed a virtualization project. In fact, about 90 percent of the workloads were running on VMware. The hardware itself was only a couple of years old.

The problem areas causing immediate concern were the Storage Array Network (SAN) and the network itself. The SAN was a brand that no one had ever really heard of, and it was pretty flaky, generating the lion's share of support tickets. The two department experts were gone, departed in the shakeup that brought me to the company in the first place. Upgrades and expansion were incredibly costly, not to mention nerve-wracking because of the seemingly delicate nature of the monster.

The network was in the midst of a conversion. Most, but not all, of the devices were Cisco and relatively new. However, some network closets around campus were a hodgepodge of older, far less reliable gear. As for the remote locations? That's where old network gear went to die. I soon learned another interesting thing about the network—we could track rainstorms better than the best

TV meteorologist just by watching which retail locations were going down!

We were running a state-of-the-art MPLS network with a major carrier in the area. Most of the sites were connected via T1s, with some of the larger sites using 10Mbs connections. The main campus was connected to the manufacturing building via a 100Mbs circuit. But "last mile" became a phrase that made the hair on the back of my neck stand up, blood vessels pop out on my temples, and my face turn beet red. The last mile was copper. When copper gets wet, network traffic halts. Our copper seemed to get wet a lot. To make matters worse, the carrier with whom we had a contract outsourced the control of the last mile to a different carrier. Ugh!

Your look in the mirror will reveal many things to you and your team. You may actually find, as I did, some functions that you had no idea your team were performing.

During our assessment, I learned a couple of things about music and its importance to the retail experience. I was invited to spend the day with our vice president of retail on what we called a "ride along." A ride along is when I would join one of the retail leaders on their rounds to visit various stores in our retail chain. It was fascinating to see the stores through their eyes, see what they saw and hear what they heard—or did not hear in this case. As we walked through one of the stores, he stopped, turned to me and said, "Listen! I don't hear the music."

"No, I don't hear it either." I started walking, thinking we would continue our walkabout.

"Do you know who I call about this?"

"Uh, Marketing?" I said with a shrug.

"No, I am pretty sure it's someone in IT."

I would later learn the music systems in the stores were the number one cause of support calls into IT, and they would soon become the bane of my existence.

Process, Process, Process

As we continued our assessment, we turned our attention to the areas of security, governance, project portfolios, business continuity and disaster recovery, and to the staff itself. There was an urban legend among the IT staffers that even though we accepted credit cards, we were not bound by the data security standards of the payment card industry. I guess because we were a non-profit. *That* went on the list to investigate.

There was not a governance process in place, no steering team, and no ticket tracking system to speak of. I was very pleased to learn there was a detailed business continuity plan with an IT disaster recovery system and both had successfully been tested the previous fall. That was one area I did not need to worry about.

The Final Grade

At the end of the eight-week period, we believed ourselves to be operating under a Silo-based model, while occasionally exhibiting traits of a Process-based Model (some processes were implemented during the assessment because they were too important to defer until after the assessment). Our report included approximately 25 "Action Areas" that would later be turned into projects. These areas ranged from applications requiring an upgrade and filling open positions to remodeling the IT area.

It had been a difficult, yet revealing, eight-week introspection of the department. However, we now knew where we were starting from. We knew our strengths, and we knew our weaknesses. We had identified and prioritized areas of risk and quick wins for improvement. We had identified projects that had the potential to deliver outstanding results for our company.

I sat down with our CEO to review the assessment before revealing it to the others on the executive team. He was surprised "we were that bad" when I explained where we were on the dial. I went on to explain that where an IT team is on the dial is neither good nor bad; it just is. It is a function of where the department believes the company wants them to be. He was very adamant; he wanted us to be operating under the Profit Generating Model. I assured him we would get there, but it would be painful, and it would take time.

We were about ready to embark on an adventure of a lifetime. Well, OK, the adventure of a career, at least. There was a ton of work to do, dozens of projects to execute, thousands of tasks to complete, so what did we do? We partied, of course! We partied like it was 2016 (apologies for the lame reference to Prince).

3

PARTY LIKE IT'S 2016!

Party like it's 2016! OK, sitting here today, that doesn't sound very prophetic, and it doesn't sound as engaging as Prince's "Party Like It's 1999." But, think about celebrating New Year's Eve 2015, ringing in the new year 2016, but it's July 2010...still not prophetic? Perhaps just a tad crazy?

One hot, steamy July Sunday afternoon in 2010, my wife Carmen and I went shopping. Have you ever tried to buy New Year's Eve decorations and party favors in July? Not an easy task! Thank goodness for Party Tree! We loaded up the car and headed downtown to my office and began to decorate the IT Conference Room (dubbed before my time the "Creativity Lab"). We had streamers, confetti, poppers, noisemakers, and, of course, a large sign: "Happy New Year 2016!" (OK, we had to make it from individual letters. Nobody, not even Party Tree, sells Happy New Year 2016 in 2010.) Once the room was complete, we locked the door and posted a sign: "Do Not Enter Until December 31, 2015," and left.

The next morning, I arrived early, my arms loaded with party snacks and bubbly (uh, it was non-alcohol, honest!). I finished setting up the room. A bit after eight o'clock, the team started to arrive. I sat in my office chuckling as I heard the buzz of curiosity make its way around the floor. Finally, nine o'clock! Time for the staff meeting! One by one, two by two, as people came in the conference room, I gave them party hats, and party favors and exclaimed, "Happy New Year 2016!" Keep in mind, I had only overseen the department for a couple of months. I am SURE they thought (and you are thinking), "This dude is CRAZY!"

Why pull off this charade? What was the point of all this wackiness? You may recall, we had just finished a very in-depth IT Assessment. This assessment had identified a couple of dozen "internal" projects the IT department needed to undertake. I was fairly certain my boss and the board of directors were not going to say, "Yeah, we know we hired you to help develop our technology strategy and leverage it to take us to the next level but go ahead and do these internal projects. We'll wait on that strategy thing for a couple of years." What we needed was a plan. A plan that incorporated those very necessary internal projects, along with business projects, along with strategic initiatives, while at the same time keeping up with the incredible pace of change in the technology space.

The Planning Begins

Where we were going would not be found on any map. We had to develop our own. My crystal ball was on the fritz, so drawing on a technique used by many professional athletes, we used visualization. I wanted our team to think about, conceptualize, and visualize what life would look like in 2016. What would business look like in 2016? What would technology look like in 2016? More specifically, what would our company look like in 2016? What would our department look like in 2016? The party was just a way to set the mood.

We spent the next hour or so brainstorming what things would look like five years from now. We could have taken a page from the *Back to the Future* trilogy and described hoverboards, power shoelaces, or, of all things, the Cubs winning the World Series (again, Cubbie fans, it was 2010; it was still several years before the curse would be broken), but we wanted something closer to reality. We filled a couple of whiteboards with ideas. Over the course of the next several months, we would vet those ideas and develop our map for the next five years.

To help draw the map, we took a three-pronged approach:

- We launched a lunch-and-learn series aimed at cross-training the team on a wide variety of topics to ensure we all had a foundational knowledge of our environment and technology.

- We created a working group to develop the processes and policies needed to become a process-oriented team with repeatable processes versus our current mostly ad-hoc state.

- We formed inter-departmental teams to not only brainstorm ideas but also build relationships throughout the organization.

Developing an IT strategic plan can be a daunting task. The assessment we had conducted was only the first part. We needed to deeply understand the company's strategic plan and each of the business unit's plans. This can prove to be difficult. In the organizations I have worked for, the corporate plan ranged from a PowerPoint presentation discussing the various markets we wanted to penetrate to a speech made by the chairman to everything in between. At Goodwill, our CEO had developed a document titled "Strategic Directions" that had then been validated by the executive team and the board.

During our IT assessment, we had met several times with each of the line of business heads. As we kicked off the strategic planning process, we armed ourselves with the Strategic Directions document and headed out to meet with them again. We wanted to gain their perspectives on what the document meant to them.

But what if your company doesn't have a strategic plan?

Driving Strategy through IT

A peer CIO, who was leading his team through a similar strategic planning process, found that his company did not yet have a strategic plan, nor could they really articulate the organizational strategy. Through a series of interviews with senior leaders, he was able to identify common threads, goals and objectives.

In order to define what IT needed to do, they first had to understand what the business as a whole was trying to accomplish. This was a new enterprise recently assembled through multiple acquisitions by a private equity firm. There seemed to be a lot of confusion about what exactly the newly formed company was trying to accomplish. It was also critical to achieve alignment amongst the senior leaders as to how they even operated, i.e. how they made money.

He proposed to the CEO that he (the CIO) should lead the top leaders of the company through a two-day session to define their new enterprise vision and strategy. This was a critical first step before any technology strategy could be created. He developed and facilitated the offsite session to define their new vision, strategic objectives, core values and key initiatives. People were each assigned an area to further develop, and follow-up sessions were required to finalize all the content. This generated lots of good discussions across the organization. Ultimately, after multiple additional sessions, the outcome was alignment on the right objectives and initiatives and clarity for everyone. This was the first time the enterprise vision and strategies for this new company had ever been documented.

Now that they had clarity on where the business was trying to go, they needed to understand how they were presently operating. They spent significant time understanding current business processes and issues and documenting high-level business workflows that had never been captured before. He recruited the entire IT organization to participate in this effort, along with many folks outside IT. This took several weeks of focused effort, and it gave everyone a baseline understanding of their current situation.

Now that they understood where they were and where they wanted to go, they needed a technology plan that would accelerate achievement of the new enterprise objectives and initiatives. Instead of focusing on technology, they could focus on solving the business problems that mattered to the company.

Governance: It Starts at the Top

As we began to get our arms around all the various things our plan should address, the process and policy working group identified a problem that needed to be rectified quickly. Their concern was the lack of governance surrounding IT. Their recommendation was to address governance even before our strategic plan was completely developed.

For example, there was no IT steering team in place. We believed to align with the needs of the business, we needed to gather the executive team together once a month to discuss progress and plans. At the time, the executive team rarely met together as a group.

I sent out an invitation to each member of the executive team. It positioned the meeting as vital to the success of IT and therefore vital to the success of the organization. Everyone accepted the invitation—everyone except one. One of the vice presidents declined to attend even the inaugural meeting. Taken somewhat aback, I reached out and scheduled a one-on-one with him to discuss.

"I don't understand the purpose of the meeting," he stated emphatically.

"Well, as I explained in my note, it is best practice for IT to be guided by a steering team, just like a company is guided by its board. The steering team becomes a sounding board. It helps decide priorities."

"Priorities? You can't tell me what my priorities are!"

"I don't mean to imply that this group will decide what your priorities are. They will help decide what *my* priorities are. With four business units and the support departments all competing for IT resources, we can't possibly do it all."

"That's why we hired you. To do it all!"

Realizing we were not getting anywhere, I tried a different tack.

"OK, so you are saying I have unlimited resources and unlimited budget to complete everyone's projects?"

"Well, obviously not."

"So, I have constraints? I have a limited budget, and I have finite resources? Let's not look at this as deciding priorities. Let's look at this as 'constraint management.' I need your help along with that of the other VPs to manage my constraints. I can't possibly understand the complexities of each department and make decisions about which projects will get what resources and in what order they will be executed. We need to have those discussions so that I can manage my constraints."

He accepted the meeting invitation.

Painting a Picture

Before we dig deeper into the development of an IT strategic plan, I'd like to discuss another of its key aspects. It must be business-focused. That may seem obvious, but I have seen way too many plans that talk only about technology and not about why the company should care. Those plans are solid, but they do not resonate with the business leaders. For the plan to be successful, it has to support the goals of the business strategic plan; it has to be clear how it supports those goals, and it has to paint a picture. To do that, you have to speak the language of business, not the language of technology.

Allow me to paint a picture from my tenure as CIO of a commercial real estate developer.

The room fell silent as I walked in. I got the feeling I had interrupted a joke or a story. It was my first time at the table. The proverbial table. The table of power. Here were gathered the ten most powerful people in our company, sans the owner himself. It was intimidating, to say the least. I was nervous. Nervous? Hell, I was scared to death.

I had 20 minutes to lay out the IT strategic plan. Twenty minutes to convince them to invest a boatload of cash. THEIR cash. Twenty minutes to convince them my strategy was the RIGHT strategy. Clutching my notes in one hand and the "clicker" in the other, I went through the slides. There were a few clarifying questions, but mostly there was silence. As I closed with my summary and stopped, all eyes were focused, not on my slides, but on me. Was this going to be the nightmare from my childhood all over again? That terrified sixth grader wanted to scream and run. Breathe. Breathe deep. Then it happened...

The president of our company leaned back in his chair, clasped his hands behind his head and said, more to me than the room, "That is the first time I have EVER understood technology!"

Suddenly, that petrified sixth grader wanted to jump for joy, wanted to slap high five with someone, anyone. Even now as I write this, I get chills. How did it happen? How did we get our point across?

An Image Takes Shape

One of my first duties as the new CIO (my first CIO role, by the way) was to develop a three-year technology strategic plan. Work on this had started before I even joined the company, with me working behind the scenes to select the third-party consulting firm as a partner in developing the plan. Once I officially started, work began in earnest.

Weeks went by. The consultant did a yeoman's job of gathering data, meeting with me and other stakeholders, working with the team to flesh out the details. Weeks turned into months. We had a lot of great stuff, but nothing was coming together. The document being produced had a lot of words; it just wasn't conveying the message. We needed something...but what? Something to pull it all together. An idea began to form.

We needed a way to convey some very complex messages to an audience that was, by their own admission, not technical. (I knew I was in trouble when one SVP looked at me during an early discussion and said, "Technology? We don't need technology. We used to design buildings with pencils and drawing paper; we can do it again.")

This was a company that made multi-million-dollar decisions every day about real estate development. How did they get comfortable with the risk versus the reward? They used a tried-and-true process. The development group would envision a project, do their research and then build what was called internally an "investment memo." The investment memo had 20 or 21 distinct sections: the executive summary, the elevation drawings, market surveys, risks, financial pro forma, and others.

What if we put the strategic plan in the form of an investment memo? We could use the analogy that configuring IT systems is like constructing a building. But no one on my team, myself included, had ever written an investment memo. We didn't even know all the sections or the lingo. I reached out to a coworker who worked in the Construction Department. He had an interest in IT and was young and passionate. Would he help me?

I flew to his hometown of Charlotte, North Carolina. He and I literally locked ourselves in my hotel room for three days. The result? A vision! A vision conveyed by images, including the image of a conceptual building, complete with elevation drawings and a pro forma. An image that everyone in the room would understand. (Thanks to Matt Cashatt for working his day job and burning the midnight oil with me for three days... and thanks to his wife for letting me impinge on their family time!)

What emerged was not only a strategic plan that spoke to the audience but our theme for the next three years:

Great People - Great Tools
Great Results

I learned many things from my time with Lauth. One of the things I learned was that before you begin to construct a building, before you have engineering drawings, before you develop site plans, you have to engage an architect to help take your vision and get it down on paper. Architecture is something the IT professional knows very well. The next step in your strategy is to turn your vision into something others can see. But before you can do that you have to be sure everyone is speaking the same language.

4

LANGUAGE MATTERS

As you may be able to discern from the discussion on how to convey your plan to others in your company, I believe language matters. The words we choose, the way we talk about technology, the way we talk about our business—words matter. To truly amplify your value, you are going to need to choose your words carefully.

One of the single biggest mistakes IT professionals make is trying to teach non-IT professionals about technology. Here is the deep, dark, dirty secret: THEY DON'T CARE! Yeah, they may go on and on about the latest "i" this or "i" that; they may come back to the office after a trip talking about an article they read about big data; they may even want to talk about home automation, but at the end of the day, they don't want to know HOW it works. They just want it to WORK.

Want to know another secret? They don't care about your service level objectives or service level agreements! Don't believe me? Try being the CIO of a retailer who experiences an outage on Black Friday. When the CEO calls, tell her, "But we have 99.9 percent uptime this year" and see how that flies. Don't get me wrong, SLAs are important, but they should be reported in business terms. Instead, report on the reduction of wait time in the checkout line, or even the number of lost sales due to long lines. That is the language that will get someone's attention.

I Think I Need an Alignment

IT professionals have been talking and fretting about "alignment with the business" for decades. There are so many things wrong with that phrase. First, let's look at the word "alignment." What does it mean to you? Dictionary.com defines "alignment," in this case, as: "a position of agreement or alliance." Agreement on what? The direction your business should take or the direction IT should take? Agreement on your priorities? Agreement with your plan?

"Alliance" is also an interesting word. Again, Dictionary.com says: "a union or association formed for mutual benefit, especially between countries or organizations." Sounds great! Can you articulate the "mutual benefit"? Are you going to form an alliance with all the leaders of the business? What if some of them have conflicting priorities or are not aligned with the others? That puts you in the middle of some interesting discussions. I've always been one to say, "If you are talking about alignment, you are not aligned."

"Alignment with the business"—what of the second half of that phrase? "The business." Aren't we all part of "the business"? One of the biggest steps you can take in amplifying your value is to become a businessman or businesswoman who understands technology instead of a technologist who knows a little bit about business. IT may not be a line of business for your company, but it is part of the business. Using the words "the business" automatically sets IT apart in the minds of the listener or reader. It puts a wall between the IT organization and the rest of the company.

Another word that drives me crazy is "user." I realize I am fighting a losing battle on this one. Dictionary. com even defines it as "a person who uses or operates something, especially computer equipment." Maybe it's because I grew up in the '60s and '70s and the word was applied to drug users. Or maybe it's all those jokes IT professionals tell during happy hour about the "idiot users." To me, the word is derogatory and negative. I try not to use it.

Throughout the years of executing our plan, the word of what to call our fellow employees who used the applications and systems we delivered evolved. As we first embarked on our journey, we wanted to instill a "great customer service" attitude throughout IT. Our reputation at the time was quite the opposite. We stayed locked in our secure area, rarely came out to see the light of day and made anyone who called the help desk feel like they were bothering us. We needed to change all that.

Building Fans

At Goodwill, we immediately began referring to "a person who uses or operates computer equipment" (i.e. everyone) as our customer. It was our first step in cranking up our value toward the Internal Service Company Model we discussed in Chapter 2. Borrowing from the Great Service Campaign that had been successful at Lauth, the IT department at Goodwill launched our own Great Service Initiative based on the Seven Steps to Great Customer Service:

1. Knowing Your Customer
2. Being Proactive
3. Follow Through Consistently
4. Communicating/Friday Call
5. Seeing Complaints as Opportunities
6. Demonstrating a Positive Attitude
7. Building Fans

The entire team went through the training. Other than a poster on the wall in the IT conference room, we didn't publicize the effort outside of IT. We wanted to see if anyone noticed a change. It wasn't long; a few weeks perhaps, and sure enough, I started to get emails from around the company commending this person or that person for helping them with some issue. After about a month or so of a concentrated effort to improve our customer service, my peers on the executive team began to notice—something was different in IT.

From User to Customer to Partner

As we continued our evolution at Goodwill, it was time to reevaluate our language again. As you recall, we were on a plan to develop the department into a Profit Generating Model and be a partner throughout the organization. That meant we needed to change our vocabulary (and our mindset once again). Referring to your co-workers throughout your organization as "customers" automatically puts you in a service provider mode. Yes, we still wanted to provide great service to our internal co-workers, but we also wanted to focus on the ultimate customers and clients of the organization. Only then could we begin to take those final steps to "partner." After hashing it out for a couple of weeks, we coined the label "Mission Partner." A Mission Partner was anyone in the Goodwill organization that did not work in IT.

When we talked about partners, we wanted to avoid the possible confusion between our internal partners throughout the business and the vendors we chose to partner with to help reach our objectives. We chose Mission Partner for our internal partners and Business Partners or Vendor Partners for the external companies we hired to accomplish some of our work. (more on that later).

A few years into my tenure at Goodwill, by way of reorganization, I was given executive responsibility for Marketing in addition to IT. I soon discovered Marketing had similar aspirations to become a partner with the other areas of the business. It wasn't just IT and it wasn't just Marketing. In fact, it was all the departments that up till then had been referred to as "the support departments." It is incredibly difficult to become a partner and earn a real seat at the table when your division name automatically puts you in a subservient role.

From that point on, I started a one-man crusade. I started referring to the departments formerly known as the support departments as the administrative division and departments.

Me, A Name I Call Myself

A final point about language: if you really want to drive home the point "life's different now" to your team and to others within your business when you embark on your strategic plan, change the name of your department. Yes, seriously!

When I arrived at Lauth, my organization was the amalgam of two previously separate departments: Enterprise Process and Information Technology. EP & IT for short. With the launch of our strategic plan, we became Enterprise Process, Information and Technology (EPI&T, or just EPIT), a subtle but important difference. First, we wanted to drop the designation of being two separate departments. Second, we felt the next phase in the evolution of commercial real estate development would be about data, and we wanted to put the "I" of Information on an equal footing with Process and Technology.

At Goodwill, our assessment revealed a poor reputation for IT throughout much of the organization. We were known as the team that said no; we were known for average or below service, and we were known for locking ourselves in our secure area and not really being a part of the business. We wanted to signal to everyone, including ourselves, life was different now. We no longer wanted to be known as the department of no; we wanted to provide solutions to our peers in the business, real solutions to their real challenges, solutions based on our expertise in technology. The Goodwill Information Technology Department became The Goodwill Technology Solutions Department or TS for short.

Language is important. The words you use can build walls or tear them down. Choose words, especially words that label, carefully. You will be amazed how fast the new language permeates your company and the difference that it makes in how others view you (and how you view yourself).

Now that you have an appreciation for the importance of language, we can turn our attention to architecture. But before you open Visio and start to draw your network diagram, let's take a different look at architecture.

5

ARCHITECTURE: THINKING BEYOND IT

" Wait, wait, wait...before we talk about all these projects, shouldn't we talk about our operating model? Are we really as diversified as we think?"

I couldn't believe my ears! I looked across the table at the EVP who had just spoken. He was the newest member of our IT steering team, and he was talking about business operating models. I nearly jumped out of my seat! *"Enterprise Architecture as Strategy!!!* You've read the book!??!" To say I was stunned would be an understatement. This EVP had barely shown an interest in anything to do with technology or IT. The only reason he was even added to the IT Steering Team was that the partners wanted him to take a more active role in other areas of the business, obviously grooming him for bigger and better things. He, almost sheepishly, replied, "I saw it in the airport bookstore yesterday and bought a copy. I'm not done reading it yet, but the first few chapters sure made a lot of sense."

I know I was stammering as I explained we had used that book as the foundation for building our IT strategic plan two years earlier. We had discussed and defined our operating model; we had designed core diagram, and we were progressing across the stages of enterprise architecture maturity. I excitedly whipped out the core diagram and began to explain the projects we were discussing in the context of the diagram. You could see the lights going on for him.

The book we were discussing, *Enterprise Architecture as Strategy*, by Jeanne Ross, Peter Weill, and David Robinson, has become my "bible" for guiding IT. While that discussion took place at a previous stop in my career, I used the same framework for developing the strategic plan at other stops in my career. In fact, it is the next step in our story. Earlier in this book, we discussed having a vision. Just like when constructing a building, to turn that vision into reality you need an architect.

Now, I will confess, I took a somewhat different approach than described in the book. The authors recommend (and I would tend to agree in different circumstances) that the leaders of the business spend time defining the operating model and discussing the core diagram. Honestly, I didn't think our leadership was ready for that type of exercise, nor did I think we had time. I was brought in to produce results, and I didn't think my boss would wait for six months while we worked through the process. Not to mention, I really take offense to the implication that IT is not "the business" and that we don't understand "the business." Would it be more effective to go through the process as a leadership team? Absolutely. But, as in the example above, it took two years before "the business" was ready to tackle something like what is described in the book.

Operating Model

The approach I took was to have my team read the book, then go through the process of defining the operating model and designing the core diagram. We didn't do it in a complete vacuum. We had countless conversations with the division heads and leaders about their specific business units. What came of this process was something just short of amazing.

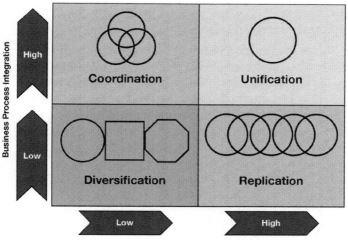

Four Operating Models

Without covering too much of the material in the book (you HAVE read it, haven't you?), there are four basic operating models of a business: Diversification, Coordination, Unification, and Replication. These are defined on a pair of axes: low to high process standardization and low to high process integration. Think about our Goodwill organization. We had four main business units. Everybody knows and loves Goodwill Retail, but we also had Commercial Services (B2B Contract Manufacturing, Warehousing, and Distribution), Education (we owned and operated charter high schools), and Community Initiatives (think mission: disability services, senior services, job placement).

Those are pretty disparate business units, to say the least. Very little process standardization and very little process integration. Must be the diversification operating model. But wait. Digging under the surface just a bit, we found an interesting set of services. For lack of a better term, we called them "Wrap-Around Services" on our Core Diagram. These services touched all the business units; they were our link.

Even with that revelation, we were still a business that, at its core, was diversified. Yet the IT Department was a centralized department, made up of generalists. Our systems approach was an ERP model versus a best of breed. Those did not seem to reconcile with what we now knew was our business model. As we continued to develop our strategic plan, we began to examine all our assumptions. Should we decentralize IT? Should we have specialists assigned to each business unit? Should we consider a best-of-breed approach?

Given the size of our department and the size of our company, we still believed there were efficiencies to be gained by keeping the department centralized. What we developed instead was a model that aligned the structure of the department to that of the business. The support model would follow the traditional Tiered Support Model, with Tier I providing that first level of support. Tier II functions would still be filled by generalists. However, when a ticket was referred to Tier III, those roles would be specific to a business division (still staffed centrally, but with domain-specific expertise).

This organizational architecture was mirrored in our systems architecture. Although we were an ERP shop, we knew our plan must allow for deviation, if not complete abandonment, of the model if the business case dictated it.

As our strategic plan began to take shape, it became clearer that the business operating model and its core diagram had impacts throughout our department, affecting everything from people and processes to systems.

It is very interesting to note, five years later, that those wrap-around services are at the very core of what the organization does. Goodwill has taken a holistic approach to helping their clients improve their economic self-sufficiency. For example, a mother in the Nurse-Family Partnership program may need to earn a high school diploma. Goodwill has a dozen high schools it owns and operates. Or there may be a student in their high schools who needs a job. Goodwill has over 3,000 jobs in its various business units. When you extend these needs beyond the individual to the family, it is easy to see how the company has evolved from a diversification business model to a coordination business model. This transformation then stimulated a metamorphosis in the IT organization and eventually the underlying systems.

The Operating Model can be a multi-layered model. While the Operating Model at Goodwill began to evolve into a Coordination Business Model, two of its business units were, at their core, replication businesses. In the retail division, the organization grew from 41 stores to 52 stores during my tenure. Today they have over 60 stores. You cannot open that many stores without being very good at replicating success. Not only do the stores have a very similar look and feel, but the underlying technology at the stores is identical. It has to be.

The same holds true in the education division, with a twist. Unlike retail stores, whose grand openings can happen throughout the year, school opens in late summer (at least in Indiana), and therefore all new locations must open at once. This places even more demands on the replication model. To open two, three and even four locations within the same week is a very complex operation. All the teams have to work in concert.

Core Diagram

The development of a Core Diagram is another essential step in not only understanding the architecture but also communicating it to business executives who may not understand complex networking diagrams. Let's dissect a couple of examples.

Lauth Group, LLC Core Diagram (circa 2007).

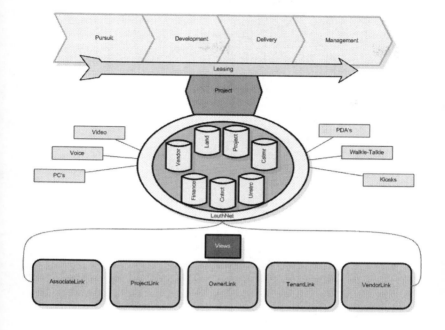

The above diagram simplifies what was a very complex set of systems and networks into a single picture. Across the top are the four major phases of the real estate development lifecycle. We could have added a fifth, Disposal, to complete the lifecycle; however, we felt it unnecessarily complicated the picture. Throughout each phase, the leasing agents worked to fill the property. Each development effort was known as a "project."

At the center of it all are the IT Systems. Here the major applications are represented by the primary types of data they control. The network ties together the primary systems, applications, and access methods.

Finally, the views provide access to the data across platforms based on the role and the relationship to the project.

What you don't see in this diagram are the product lines of Retail, Healthcare, Office, and Industrial. While there are differences in how a healthcare building is designed and built and how a retail mall is designed and built, there is little difference in the actual process by which the development is carried out. What appeared to be a Diversification Model going in really turned out to be a Unification Model. That revelation plays out in the Core Diagram.

Goodwill Industries of Central Indiana circa 2010.

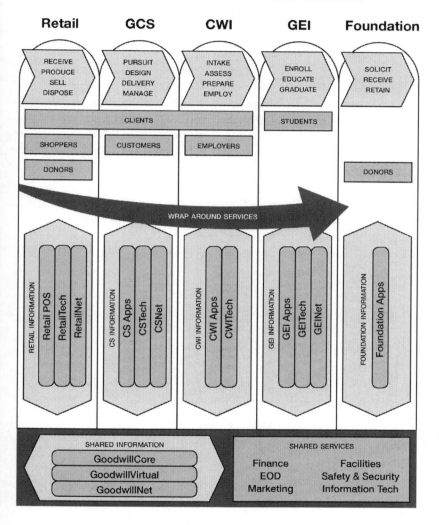

As can be seen in Goodwill's diagram, there are four very distinct business units and the Foundation. The processes described across the top are different for each one.

There are some commonalities in the constituents the business units serve, but there is certainly more variation than commonalities.

In the center, the business units use applications central to them. Each one is using best-of-breed applications to deliver their services; each one has their own "source of truth" to the data. As I mentioned in a previous chapter, the organization had just implemented an ERP system when I joined, prior to the launch of the strategic planning process. The initial business units on the ERP included Finance and Commercial Services. The intent was to roll out the ERP to the other BUs. I can't help but think: if they had a view of the business using the Operating Model and the Core Diagram, they would not have made the decision to start down the ERP path. It was a decision that was challenged with the very next BU to upgrade its software, but more on that later.

At the bottom of the Core Diagram are the supporting departments and the supporting systems. These systems included the intranet, website, and the WAN. All of these departments and systems were used throughout the organization by each BU to deliver its service to its clients.

And that arrow across the middle? As I mentioned earlier in this chapter, during our strategic planning process, we identified some services that were being performed in the BUs that were cross-functional (or needed to be). At the time, we didn't know where to put them, so we encircled the BUs with "Wrap Around Services."

Communication Tools

The Core Diagrams are a tool, a tool to facilitate conversation. When you meet with a business leader, take the Diagram with you. As they describe a problem, issue, or vision, you can use the diagram to show them where it fits into the overall architecture of the business itself, how it impacts the other departments, and how it impacts other applications and systems. It gives you a common language to use when discussing complex technology systems.

Talk architecture to most IT professionals and you get a complex set of Visio diagrams that show how the switches and routers are connected or how the various systems are connected. Perhaps some have drawn diagrams to show how the applications "talk" to each other. I believe to get an adequate view of the business you need at least five layers of architectural "drawings."

- The Business Architecture using the Operating Model and Core Diagram
- The Business Process Architecture
- The Information/Data Architecture using Data Diagrams to show the relationship between the data
- The Application Architecture using Application Dependency Mappings
- The Network Architecture using Network and Systems Diagrams

By now, you have a vision, you have a common language, and you have tools to help you communicate. It's time to begin to put it all together using the strategic plan framework.

6

WHAT WOULD AN IT
BOOK BE WITHOUT A
FRAMEWORK?

I n Chapter 2 we discussed the need to write your
strategic plan in a way that resonates within your
business. At Lauth, we used the analogy of developing a commercial building. We even went so far as to
format the plan like an investment memo, a group of
documents used to evaluate a development decision at
the firm.

At Goodwill, we used a similar analogy because of
the pace at which new retail locations and schools were

opened. However, we did slant our design toward the look and language of the Strategic Directions document familiar to leadership.

The CIO of a law firm might use the analogy of a legal brief, tying the development of the plan and the execution of the plan to processes used to develop and build a legal case. The CIO might also approach the entire process like a negotiation. The managing partners and the other attorneys will feel comfortable in the context of a negotiation process, mitigating risk.

The image or analogy you choose may dictate the sequence of the content in your plan, but there are some key elements your plan should cover.

Introduction

This section is perhaps the most important. In the introduction, you paint the picture; you create the image. The image must be vivid enough to catch the attention of the reader. As you paint the picture, you also answer the "why" and the "how." Your "why" is your vision. Why do you do what you do? Why is it important to your business? Your "how" are your strategies. How are you going to achieve your vision? Which strategies will keep you on the path? Speak to the decision-makers in the language that resonates with them. You will need their support so you can execute the "what." What specific things are you going to do within the strategies to obtain your vision?

Current State

Think of this section as an executive summary of the department assessment you performed before launching the strategic planning process. Pull out the salient points from the assessment. Remember, you are still painting a picture. This section helps to support the "why." Allow the reader to "see" the impacts of status quo.

It is important to cover the current state of the market in which the business operates, the business itself, technology, the technology currently leveraged by the business, and the department resources and structure.

Enterprise Architecture

In the Lauth strategic plan, we called these the "Elevations." In the world of construction, elevations are the drawings of the building being contemplated. For the purpose of your plan, this is where you describe the business's operating model and reveal (and explain) your core diagram.

Thorough, collective comprehension of these aspects are paramount to your plan's success. Take the time now to ensure everyone understands the Operating Model and Core Diagram. If needed, make changes based on the feedback you receive to make them even clearer.

Vision, Mission, Governance and Core Principles

Define your department's mission and vision. This relates to the "what." What do you want the IT department to become, and how does that vision relate to the corporate vision? The mission is the "how." How will IT partner with the other departments to deliver on the departmental vision and, more importantly, the corporate vision?

Lay out your governance structure. How will technology decisions be made? Who makes them? Is there a steering team? How will it operate?

Core principles are the guardrails. They help you and your team make decisions in the "heat of the battle." They are agreed upon through the governance structure. Any deviation from the core principles must be contemplated with care, and the impacts of the deviation fully understood. These deviations should be wrestled with through the governance structure as well. We will cover some examples of this process later in the book.

Recent Improvements

You haven't been standing still while you've been developing your strategic plan, right? Here is where you let the world know all the great things you have already accomplished. Often, these are process improvements, but they can also be projects that have been completed. Any work done to stabilize the systems and network should be called out here as well.

In short, brag. Part of running an IT department strategically is marketing the department to the rest of the organization. Celebrate your successes. Think of it like issuing a press release for each completed project.

Roadmap

This is the meat of the plan. Here you lay out the projects and initiatives you need to complete to take you from point A to point B. The roadmap should be divided into short-term (under a year), mid-term (1 to 2 years) and long-term (beyond two years). The further out you go, the less concrete these ideas will be. In keeping with the image you created in your introduction, consider naming the projects within the same theme. For example, at Lauth, we labeled the three time horizons as: Delivery,

Development, and Pursuit. Some of the project names included Conduit, Cornerstone and Yellow Brick Road (OK, that name might have been a bit of a stretch, but it sure paints a picture).

Conclusion

This is your close, your final pitch, your "ask." Here you tie it all together. To use the parlance of public speaking: in the introduction, you "tell 'em what you are going to tell 'em," then "you tell 'em," finally, in the conclusion, you "tell 'em what you told 'em." Make it a strong finish.

Others

Other sections can also add to your story and support your plan. They could include: Executive Summary, Budget (if not covered in the Roadmap), Trends (business, industry and technology), and Benchmarks (compare against others in your industry).

You will find an outline of this framework in the resources section at the end of this book or online at www.JeffreyTon.com/AmplifyYourValue/Resources.

A Word to the Future CIO

By now you may be thinking this is a pretty big stretch. The head of IT laying out a business vision, a new technological path, and asking for a big chunk of change to get it done. You may not feel you have the creativity to develop the image that connects the dots for the executive team.

The skills you will need to lead this transformation, and the skills that great CIOs possess are: seeing the big picture *through* the lens of the business and the ability to take risks (educated risks though they may be). They need a foundation in project management and organizational change management, as well as a belief in standards and process (and the guts to break them when needed).

Oh yeah, you will also need to be tech-savvy. What do I mean by that? It's been a long time since I wrote any software, tore apart a PC, or even installed a new application (uh, except on my phone), yet I understand technology and how businesses can use technology to further their business. I keep abreast of new tech, not to be attracted by the bright shiny object, but always with the lens of "how could my business use this new widget, and will it make an impact?"

7

WE NEED TO
TALK PROCESS
IMPROVEMENT

Maybe it was the state of the organizations I walked into throughout my career, or maybe it is because processes can always be improved. Regardless, some of the quickest wins I have achieved were in the area of process improvement.

In the strategic plan framework, almost always the "Recent Improvements" section details the implementation of new processes or the refinement of existing ones. These processes were identified during the Current State Assessment by comparing current processes (or lack thereof) against the ITIL framework.

Some of these need to be attacked right away and should not wait until your full strategic plan is complete. In the Recent Improvements section, you can declare victory in those areas and (hopefully) report progress in others. In the departments I have had the privilege of leading, as well as those I have consulted with, the three processes that have almost always risen to the top to be addressed first were: Root Cause Analysis, Project Approval, and Change Management.

Each of these can have a profound impact on your team and the way it is viewed throughout the organization and, with the exception of Project Approval, are relatively easy to implement. If your team is experiencing stability issues throughout the technical environment, developing and implementing a Root Cause Analysis (RCA) process is the quickest way to stabilize the environment. It has the added benefit of sending the message throughout your business that you take the issues seriously.

Root Cause Analysis

The RCA should include a description of the issue, the business impact of the issue, a description of the underlying cause or causes, what actions were taken to repair the issue and what actions are to be taken to prevent a recurrence of the issue. Here is where transparency and honesty can pay off. If the underlying cause was an action your team took, say that. Don't sweep it under the rug, but don't throw someone under the bus either. Remember, you succeed as a team and you fail as a team.

The key is to allow the team the time it takes to understand the cause. "We don't know" is rarely a comforting answer to those impacted by an outage. As you continue to ask your team "why," they will, in turn, begin to ask why.

Once "why" is answered, the next question is "How can it be prevented?" This may be a new way of thinking for many on your team. They have probably gotten very good at fixing the symptoms but taking the time to understand the cause and putting systems or processes in place to prevent the recurrence of the issue might be foreign. Be ready for "But it's faster just to fix it when it happens than to make the changes to keep it from happening" excuse.

I've mentioned the music in retail stores elsewhere in this book. It was far "easier" to have the store manager reboot the on-site device to restart the music than it was to investigate what was causing the device to stop in the first place. It took months of troubleshooting, reviewing logs, and updating firmware before we found that the app we were using to drive the music was prone to lock up if its buffer overflowed. By replacing the app with a more robust version, we were able to virtually eliminate the "sounds of silence" in the stores.

Change Management

That leads us to the next process that can add some sanity to your life: Change Management. Establish a team of subject matter experts from your department and have that team review changes to your production environment. If the department has never had a Change Management process, be ready for pushback.

"Do you mean we have to wait a week to receive approval to make a change?"

"I can't possibly document every change I make."

"This is just going to slow us down."

Yes, these complaints and many more are in your future. However, implementing Change Management can dramatically reduce "shooting yourself in the foot" errors, foster communication throughout your team, and enable faster triage in the event an issue does arise out of the change. The trick is to define what changes must go through the process, what constitutes an emergency change, and how much documentation is needed for the change.

I like to start by keeping it simple. ALL changes to the production environment, with the exception of partner (er, uh, end-user) account adds, changes or deletes come to the Change Management meeting. As the team's maturity increases, you can determine the different types of changes and what level of change management is required for each one.

The need for emergency changes will never go away completely. Frequent Change Management meetings can reduce emergency changes, but unless you meet daily (which I don't recommend) you will still need to contend with some volume of these changes. You will need to define what an emergency change is and what process is followed when one needs to be made. We tried to make it simple. If waiting until the next change management meeting would cause more harm than the risk of making the change that's called for, an emergency change is warranted. Yes, its use is still a judgment call, and yes, the process is still open to abuse.

For example, to make an emergency change at Goodwill required approval from next level management, at the very least. Depending upon the potential impact, it could require CIO approval. Giving changes that visibility in and of itself reduces the number of emergency changes. If the change required manipulation of application data, business owner approval was also needed.

The change must still be documented and presented to the Change Management Team after the fact. In addition to reviewing what was done and determining if an RCA was warranted, the team should also weigh in on whether or not it was, in fact, an emergency change.

Project Approval

The third process that has identified itself time and time again in the early stages of moving the needle on departmental maturity and transformation is the Project Approval process. This is a little more difficult to implement because it will require participation and support from the other business units. To get the ball rolling, you will need to take two seemingly easy steps. First, define a project. Next, gather a list of all active projects.

The Project Management Institute defines a project as: "...a temporary endeavor undertaken to create a unique product, service or result. A project is temporary in that it has a defined beginning and end in time, and therefore defined scope and resources." Your definition should start there. However, because of the amount of effort involved in tracking and reporting on a project, you should also add a level-of-effort component to it. In other words, the effort may be a project in the purest sense, but if the level of effort to complete it is under 40 hours (or 80 hours, or whatever number makes sense for your team), we aren't going to treat it as a project, we are going to manage it as a task.

Once you have definition of a project, you can start to create the list of active projects, AKA the Project

Portfolio. This process can take some digging. During the initial stages of our transformation at Goodwill, we identified over 80 "active" projects. I use quotes because you and I both know with a team of 20 people, there is no way to manage 80 active projects. No wonder our partners in the business felt like we never got anything done! It certainly led to some lively debate at the next IT Steering Team meeting.

The simple steps of 1) defining a project, 2) gathering your list of projects and 3) exposing the list to your newly formed IT Steering Team will set a solid foundation for implementing a project request and approval process.

Incident and Request Management

Once you have addressed these first three processes, it's time to tackle the elephant in the datacenter: Incident and Request Management. These can typically be addressed simultaneously because the workflows (at least at a high level) are the same. When someone in the business needs work from IT, they request it, IT prioritizes then schedules the work, and IT completes the work. This work could be a new service (Request) or to repair something that is not functioning (Incident).

What is key in this process is to capture the requests in a central location so they can be managed. This means either the person needing the work completed or someone in IT must enter the request into whatever tracking system you are using. This will be one of the most challenging aspects of implementing these workflows and will call upon all of your organizational change management skills. More on that in a moment.

I've always used the traditional Tiered Support Model. Tier I handles all the inbound requests. They categorize and prioritize the request, perform triage, and attempt resolution. Tier II handles the incidents and requests referred by Tier I. Tier III handles the referrals from Tier II. Rarely was Tier IV needed. In many cases, Tier IV was a vendor or supplier. In this model, each Tier has the responsibility to document what was done to complete the work with the goal of enabling the lower Tier to complete the work in the future.

When I arrived at Goodwill, they were not using the tiered model. Each of the 2,500 employees who needed work completed by IT would either call a central number or the direct line of someone they knew in IT, send an email to someone they knew in IT, or grab someone from IT in the hallway. Most of the time the central number was not used, but when it was, the phones on a handful of IT pros' desks would ring, and whoever was not busy would pick up the phone. No one was allowed into the IT area, and the IT staff rarely left the area.

The posted hours for IT were 7:30 AM to 5:30 PM. Outside of those hours, the central number would roll over to voicemail, and the caller would have to leave a message. The voicemail system would page (yes, page) whoever was on-call. The on-call person would have to call into the voicemail, retrieve the message, and then call the person needing the work completed.

This process only worked so well. It was predicated on the fact that when the on-call person returned the call, the person needing the work was sitting by the phone waiting for the call. Have you ever worked in retail? If you have, you know. Rarely do you have any time to wait by the phone. Yes, most of the time this process turned into one long game of telephone tag.

Our retail stores were open seven days a week (IT worked Monday through Friday). The stores were open until 9 PM (IT worked until 5:30). Around this same time, we were opening our first high school for adults, called the Excel Center. Guess what they offered? Evening classes, which meant more mission partners working beyond our help desk hours.

We were using a homegrown ticketing system to track the requests and the incidents. But something wasn't jibing in my head. As I reviewed the past two years of monthly reports, I took note of the number of tickets reported: 297, 311, 291, 295, 304, 325... Roughly, an average of 300 tickets a month for a company of 2500+ employees? Only 10 each day for a staff of 20? Something wasn't adding up; this team was far busier than that.

Tiered Support

Tackling all of these problems at once would take months. Rather than eating the elephant whole, we started with a couple of small bites. First, we implemented a Tiered Support model. The roles and responsibilities of each tier were defined. We limited whose phone would ring when someone called the help desk to the desktop support staff only. They were deemed Tier I. Whoever answered the phone owned the ticket. They were responsible for entering it into the ticketing system, in addition to the initial triage.

We assigned each of the desktop support staff to a specific business unit. They were responsible for learning and understanding the applications and the major business functions of their business unit. What this meant was if a retail clerk called the help desk, any of the five desktop-support specialists would answer the phone, as Tier I. If they were unable to resolve the issue, it was referred to Tier II. If the desktop support specialist who answered the phone was assigned to retail, they would handle BOTH the Tier I role and the Tier II role on that ticket. If, instead, they were assigned to education, they would perform the Tier I role and then refer it to the Tier II retail specialist.

This achieved two things. First, it created accountability for entering the ticket into the tracking system. Second, the team began to learn more about the specific business units, allowing them to solve more tickets. That first month the number of tickets jumped to over 500. Were there more incidents? No—more were being entered.

24x7x365 Done Right

We could not solve the coverage hours issue without adding personnel to the department. Rather than doing that, we turned to Netfor, a local IT Service Desk company. They provided 24 x 7 x 365 coverage, the discipline of a commercial call center, and the tools of a commercial call center. They would handle Tier I. Any ticket not solved on the first call would be referred to the in-house team as Tier II. Incident volume again jumped, this time to over 1,300.

More tickets were being entered, which provided more data to understand underlying issues. Immediately, the team was no longer tied to their phones. They were now able to be out and visible, learning more about the business, identifying ways they could proactively prevent issues before they started.

Through Netfor, we could now implement Problem Management, tie related issues together and resolve the real problem, not just the symptoms. The more procedures we documented, the higher their first-call resolution became. We began to average almost 80 percent first-call resolution. We could also identify long-term nagging problems and fix them once and for all. Remember that music problem in the stores? Once the number one cause of tickets, it is now a thing of the past.

Did we reduce the number of desktop support specialists? No! Our systems engineers, network engineers, and application developers, who acted in the role of Tier III, began to document the issues they resolved, enabling the Tier II technicians to resolve more issues, reducing the number referred to Tier III. These higher-priced resources could now spend more time on projects, moving the business forward at an even faster pace.

Over time, Netfor became even more ingrained in the business of Goodwill, handling not only the IT tickets but the consumer calls on the Rewards Card, the scheduling of donation home pickups and employee HR and benefit calls.

Other processes we defined and implemented during the initial stages of our strategic plan included Purchasing, Password Policy, Email Retention, Hardware & Software Standards, and a Technology Refresh Policy.

Core Principles

A key document I have used throughout my career is one I call "Guiding Principles" or "Core Principles." Not really a process or procedure, this list covers the major components of managing an IT department and ties them back to the company's core principles. Let me give you some examples.

Application Portfolio Core Principles

Principle: We seek Enterprise Resource Planning (ERP) solutions that are either part of the core ERP or that integrate well and provide uniform solutions across business units.

Amplification: Given the Company's business model, it is important to have a core system that can be leveraged across the various business units. To gain further efficiencies and standardized data, we will look first to the ERP functionality and, where possible, adjust the business process to fit the core. Where this is not possible, we will seek solutions that integrate well into the core and share common infrastructure.

Why it is important: one of the major guiding principles of managing a portfolio of IT assets is the decision of "ERP vs. Best-of-Breed." Stating we are an ERP shop dramatically narrows the scope of possible solutions to solve a business problem. For example, if the company is an ERP shop and needs to replace its Point-of-Sale system, the first solution to be reviewed is the one offered by the ERP vendor or within the ERP vendor's ecosystem of add-on modules.

Technology Infrastructure Core Principles

Principle: We will manage the use of non-Company-owned devices for the purpose of performing Company business by protecting and controlling the Goodwill information and by protecting the Goodwill Network.

Amplification: Supporting personal computing devices such as laptops, cell phones, printers and other such items can be extremely expensive and can present a risk to the Company computing systems. The Company IT Standards Process will define the standard equipment and the process by which the standard can be amended. With the advent of PDAs, smartphones, and other personal computing devices, rather than restrict their use, we will focus on data and network protection while providing limited support of these devices.

Why it's important: As IT, your first responsibility is to protect the company data and network. In a bring-your-own-device, consumer-technology-driven world, it becomes difficult, if not impossible, to support every make and model of smartphone, for example.

Investment Core Principle

Principle: We purchase systems rather than custom develop our own systems unless a quantified competitive advantage can be proven.

Amplification: Competitive advantage includes timing, migration cost, maintenance, support, and entry barriers. Given our ERP foundation, we will seek software that interacts with the following systems, in the following order:

- ERP Core Modules (Microsoft A
- Core Applications (Microsoft RMS
- Portal Applications (SharePoint

- Software-as-a-Service Applications
- Custom Develop (Using our Standard Platform)

Why it's important: Another one of IT's basic tenets is Build vs. Buy. As a Buy shop, you can lean on the software provider for some level of support. It helps to focus and narrow the scope of choices when trying to solve a business problem.

All of these principles act as a guide when making decisions, not only in the day to day but also in the mid- and long-term. If the team deviates from these principles, this should trigger referral to the CIO and probably to the IT Steering Team. The full impact of deviating from these principles must be understood by all the decision-makers before rendering their decision.

You will find a full example of these core principles in the Resources section at the end of this book, or online at: www.JeffreyTon.com/AmplifyYourValue/Resources.

By now you've assessed your department, defined your vision, identified a myriad of projects and initiatives, implemented some governance, and started process improvement. In some ways, you have already moved into the execution phase, but now it's time to step on the gas!

WE INTERRUPT THIS

PROGRAM...

We interrupt this program to bring you this special announcement. Whether you are a new CIO or have been in the role for some time, when you develop your strategic plan, you will have funding requests. Implementing your plan will take investment. In fact, your first-year budget probably will raise eyebrows. Be ready for it.

At Goodwill, we had already embarked on the initial stages of the plan. About a year in, it was time for the normal budget cycle. Time to submit the budget for year two of the plan. The proposed budget flew through the internal approvals. However, when it got to the Audit and Finance Committee of the Board, it became a different story.

You may recall that earlier in this book, I talked about the reaction of the CEO at my prior company when we unveiled the plan. The reaction this time was a bit different. While the committee was generally supportive of the ideas, they provisionally approved the budget with one caveat. One of the directors suggested we hire a third party to assess the plan and validate the direction. After all, no one on the board really understood technology, he said.

At first, I was taken aback. "How dare they second-guess me? Isn't this why they hired me? Don't they trust me?" By the time I made it back to my office, I had gathered myself. Of course, they trusted me, but these were big dollars. If I were a CFO, my work would get audited every year. This would be no big deal. I knew the plan was rock solid.

I reached out to the local office of Resources Global Professionals. Not only had I worked for them myself, doing just this kind of assessment, but they had acquired the firm my previous company had used to develop their IT strategic plan. Within a couple of weeks, they had a consultant on the ground who looked everything over, interviewed department heads, discussed the plan with the IT team and wrote his report to the board. He agreed, the plan was rock solid. He did make a couple of recommendations related to timing on some of the initiatives, but nothing substantial. In the end, the board approved the budget.

Be ready for it!

Now, back to our regularly scheduled programming...

EXECUTING THE STRATEGY

8

THAT PROJECT IS A REAL CLUSTER

S NAFU, FUBAR, CF... If you have been in IT longer than five minutes, you have been involved in a
project that has been described as a real cluster. (If
you are confused, look it up in the Urban Dictionary).

In fact, these words are used so often to describe IT
projects, when one of the panelists at a recent MIT Sloan
CIO Symposium said, "You know, there are two types
of IT projects: A-C and C-F," the room of IT executives exploded in laughter, many of them shaking their
heads and shuddering as if having flashbacks of projects
past, nightmares of projects present, or trepidations of
projects future.

"No, no, no, I'm not talking about THAT kind of C-F project. I'm talking about a grading scale. Let me explain. There are some projects that no matter how well you execute them, no matter if you hit the ball out of the park, the best grade you will ever receive is a 'C'. No one is ever going to walk into your office, shake your hand and say, 'Thank you for delivering my email today.' No one ... EVER. On the other hand, if the project goes poorly or if email goes down, you will most certainly receive an 'F' (and you WILL be in a 'cluster' of a situation). Conversely, there are some projects that when executed properly will garner you rave reviews and most certainly earn you an 'A'. When those projects miss the mark a bit, you can earn a 'B' or even a 'C'."

As the panel continued its discussion on stage, their words faded into the background, and I thought about what I had just heard. He was *right!* I started thinking about all the projects on our plate. I would categorize most of them as 'C-F' projects. The speaker had even called out the biggest project facing us at the moment— email. We were faced with another massive upgrade of our email system. It would take months and tens of thousands of dollars. And in the end? We would still be delivering email. It was an epiphany. Why on earth would we ever want to go down that road again, and again and again? I'd like to say it was a Cecil B. DeMille moment and the heavens parted, the sun shone down, a rainbow formed, and a booming voice said, "Cloud!" but honestly, it was more like a quiet whisper inside my head. "Cloud ... move the C-F work to the cloud."

Before my colleagues and I even returned from the conference, we pulled up the project portfolio we had developed during the strategic planning process. We started looking at the projects in a new light, categorizing all of our projects and assigning them to one of three categories: maintain (C-F projects), grow (BC projects) and innovate (AB projects).

Now, this approach is nothing earth-shattering. IT departments across the globe categorize their projects in the same way. The difference for us was our approach to the C-F projects. For each one, we asked, "Is there a better way?" Could someone else do these projects, and if so, could this eliminate some of the "keeping the lights on" work that is the bane of those same IT departments? In other words, could the work be moved to the cloud?

A-C vs. C-F Projects

The day after our return, we met with the rest of the IT leadership team. Together, we reviewed the categorization we'd completed on the plane. We moved some things around based on their input. We then turned our attention to those C-F projects. The dozen projects included some pretty hefty items:

- Exchange Upgrade
- SAN Controller Upgrade
- VMWare Upgrade
- DR Hardware Refresh
- Production Hardware Refresh

If I ever saw a list of projects that had the potential to be real C-F projects, this was it.

We will discuss our cloud strategy later, but for now, suffice it to say, we looked to the cloud to outsource as much of the C-F work as we could.

Slowly at first, and then faster and faster, we were able to divert more of our resources (human and financial) to growth and innovation. To me, *that* is the true promise of cloud: moving the needle from 80 percent maintenance to 70 percent, 60 percent...and lower. Sure, it can save some money, but what it really does is make you more agile and elastic. You can quickly focus your talent on business initiatives that are truly game-changers, not just another hardware or software upgrade.

Together, the IT Team, along with the IT steering team, began to map out our journey, our journey into the unknown.

Draw Your Own Map

The day was blistering hot. The air did not move. It was stifling. The crowd gathering in this Kansas field struggled to find shade. Several people stood in the shadows of the tall grasses surrounding the field. Sweat poured off of me, even though I was standing still. I didn't even want to fan myself because that would be too much exertion.

It was July 4th, 2004. My wife, Carmen, and I were standing in this field, nearing heat stroke, to commemorate the 200th anniversary of the Lewis and Clark Expedition passing through this area. (Yes, in addition to loving IT, I love history! I am SUCH a nerd!) OK, I can hear you, "What does this have to do with amplifying your value, much less IT? I am pretty sure they didn't have computers in 1804!" Bear with me for a few more paragraphs, dear IT explorer ...

After standing through several speeches and re-enactments, we piled back into busses for the ride back to Atchison. On the bus, we could put the windows down and get a breeze, but we were packed in like sardines. The sweat continued. I felt sorry for the two women whose seat we were sharing.

We poured out of the bus like water bursting through a dam and headed straight to a local bar and grill for lunch and a cold one, or two or three. There they were, posters everywhere. We had to try one; Boulevard Brewing Co. (https://www.boulevard.com/) was a sponsor of the Lewis & Clark Event. The slogan: "For those who make maps, not follow them."

Think about that—"For those who make maps, not follow them." That is the definition of an explorer. Two centuries ago they would "step off the map," going where no American had ever gone before.

Our IT department at Goodwill had been on a journey. We had looked inward to see where we were; we had looked forward to envision the future; we had studied our business and identified the impacts it had on our organization, and we had decided we wanted to do value-add projects to the best of our abilities. Like Lewis and Clark, we were then stepping into the unknown. There was no map for where we were going. We were blazing trails.

It may seem at odds with the intent of this book to say I am not drawing a map for you to follow. What I hope to accomplish is to teach you cartography—the art of drawing your own map. Yes, you have to follow some of the steps we have discussed. But, your actual road-map will differ greatly from ours. That is OK and to be expected. Businesses are different, cultures are different, and environments are different. The point here is, if you have followed the steps, you now know where you are, and you know where you are going.

Like Lewis and Clark 200 years ago, we had a goal. We had an objective. To draw our map, we identified immediate steps we needed to take. Lewis and Clark needed specific skill-sets; they needed discipline, and they needed teamwork and collaboration. We needed process; we needed education, and we needed different skills. We needed a deeper understanding of our mission. We identified many of the steps required to make our journey ahead successful. Like good IT professionals, we identified dependencies and precursors to our journey. We laid out a five-year plan.

Five years is eons in the IT world. Perhaps it was too much of a chunk to bite off from where we were. The first year or two were very specific. We had processes we wanted to execute; we had technologies we wanted to implement, and we had an ever-evolving business that we needed to support and lead. Like Lewis and Clark before us, we did not bind ourselves to specifics in a future we could not foresee. Had they not been open and flexible, they never could have traveled to the Pacific Ocean and returned to "civilization." We laid out specific steps in the near-term and specific goals in the long-term. Each year we reviewed our plan and we adjusted our steps, but we did not adjust our strategy or our vision.

I have to admit, some of the pieces of our journey just fell into place. Sometimes it is better to be lucky than good. We were able to invest in new Disaster Recovery technology because our prior investments all hit their depreciation at the same time. We were able to migrate our production environment, for pretty much the same reason. However, there were many times on our journey that we had to adjust, ad-lib, step off the map we had drawn. As you learn more, as you experience more, you need to be flexible and adjust your tactics to meet your objectives.

Your journey will not be the same as ours. Your company is different; your culture is different. Technology is different. You have to be willing to step into the unknown. You have to be willing to draw your own map. You have to be willing to keep your focus on the mission and the destination and adjust your plan to reach that destination. Make your own map.

But to throw in just one more obscure reference: *Patience, Grasshopper.* Follow the rest of our journey and your path will become clear.

9

LATHER, RINSE, REPEAT

We all know a strategic plan of any kind shouldn't just be put on a shelf to gather dust, right? We know that, right? A key to the success of your strategic plan is to keep it evergreen. Things change, and quickly. Technology evolves at the speed of light (or so it seems). You have to be able to react to changes in technology, changes in your business, and changes in your industry.

I wrote a blog post several years ago titled, "The Problem with Roadmaps." One of the problems, I opined, was that roadmaps are static, and were especially so back in the days of paper maps. However, even in this modern digital age, we sometimes ignore the signs of change around us and cling to the plan.

Several months ago, I was leaving my office to head downtown to a new restaurant. I, of course, knew how to get downtown: head west on 71st Street, take I-465 south to I-65 South. What I didn't know was the best exit to take and how to navigate to the restaurant from the Interstate. I went ahead and fired up my trusty Google Maps and headed out. But something was strange; Google was telling me to go straight on 71st Street all the way to I-65, skipping the shortcut of I-456 to I-65. "Why the heck would it tell me that?" I asked myself.

Thinking I knew better than the stupid technology, I jumped on I-465 southbound. I hadn't even gotten off the ramp yet when I saw it: a backup as far as the eye could see. I spent the next 45 minutes crawling the two miles to the I-65 exit, with no way to backtrack. Ugh! Environments change. Circumstances change. We have to be ready to adapt our plan (and sometimes even our strategy). To do that, you have to be intentional.

Annual Planning and Strategy Refinement

Not wanting to jerk the team around by reviewing and second-guessing our strategy and plan constantly, we made it a point to review both at least annually. (We reserved the right to call an audible during the year, however, if external factors warranted it.) I had long used an annual retreat with my direct reports to review our success, learn from our failures and lay out a plan for the year ahead. Typically, this would occur a month or so before the kick-off of the budget cycle.

In this setting, we would review the strategy, including the core principles. It almost took on the flavor of a new strategic planning process but in a condensed two-day offsite event. We reviewed trends and business plans to identify shifts or wholesale changes of direction and how they might impact our strategy and roadmaps.

Most were minor tweaks, such as flipping the priority of a couple of projects based on increasing or diminishing business needs. Occasionally, we would encounter a 180-degree change of direction, requiring not only a change to the plan but to one of the core principles. Case in point was the selection of a new HRIS that was not a module within our ERP system. In that one decision, we shifted from an ERP shop to a best-of-breed shop. I will talk more about that in a subsequent chapter.

Taking Your Vendors for the Ride

As we were about to enter the second year of our plan, I added a new twist to our offsite retreat. I invited our vendors to participate. Before you put down this book in the face of such heresy, let me give you the method to my madness and the talk about how this evolved over the years. I think implementing something similar can make a significant difference in the success of your plan.

The word "partner" gets thrown around a lot in the world of IT. Every vendor that walks in the CIO's door wants to be her partner. "We would really like to be your partner" many times is code for "We really want to sell you something." However, the CIO is just as guilty. We want vendors that will partner with us. But what does that mean? A vendor who will share in the risk as well as the reward? I think it goes well beyond contractual arrangements.

Like a marriage, a partnership requires 100 percent from both parties, not 50 percent. If I want vendors who will treat me as a partner, I need to treat them as partners. That means building a relationship built on trust, respect, and transparency, with common goals. Trust, respect, and transparency that go both ways at 100 percent.

Earlier in my career, I was involved in a large outsourcing project. We were moving all of our application development work offshore to India. As we began to implement the transition plan with the vendor, the subject of culture came up. I asked if there was going to be an opportunity to learn and understand the culture of the offshore staff. The vendor assured me there was no need. We didn't need to learn their culture; they would learn ours.

Two months into the transition to the outsourcer, the lack of communication was obvious: missed deadlines, code that did not match specifications, designs that were nowhere close to acceptable. I realized how wrong they were about the need to understand their culture. To make this work, we had to understand and respect each other's culture. My team and I packed our bags and headed out to experience it firsthand. This made a huge difference in understanding, built relationships (some that still exist today) and opened up a level of communication that could not otherwise have been possible.

"I want fewer vendors and more partners" become my mantra.

Put On Your Big Boy/Girl Pants

As we prepared for our first retreat with our vendors, we reviewed the list of vendors we used. We identified the ones with whom we had the largest spends, and they were invited. Invitations were issued. Two people from each company could attend. There might be competitors in the room. That's OK. We were here for the purpose of advancing Goodwill's strategic plan. Period. No selling.

My team was to meet for a day and half at a hotel and conference center in Nashville, Indiana. The idea was to not only get away from the office but also get out of town. The vendor partners were invited to join us after lunch on the second day for an afternoon of discussion. One of the vendors volunteered to sponsor dinner afterwards.

This initial summit was really all about us. What I mean by that was, we presented to the vendors. We told the Goodwill story, we discussed our business, and we discussed our IT strategic plan. We then recapped the prior day and a half of discussion and asked for feedback.

As you might imagine, the feedback got off to a slow start. Trust had not been built yet. Many in the room did not know all the Goodwill team, much less each other (see previous point about competitors). Slowly but surely, most of the attendees began to provide feedback... excellent feedback.

Not Quite a Blood Oath

We ended the day with a ceremony. Borrowing from something I had seen when visiting another Goodwill organization, we created a Mission Wall. They had printed copies of their organization's mission statement. All of the employee in the department signed their names. They had the statements framed and hung on the wall. It was a constant reminder of the employees' commitment to the mission.

We passed out two copies of a certificate to each attendee, including the vendor partners. Each of the certificates had the Goodwill mission statement, but rather than "Goodwill," it used the person's name. For example,

> I, Jeff Ton, offer opportunities, provide services, and leverage my resources with those of others to improve the education, skills, employability, and economic self-sufficiency of adults and the future employability of young people.

At the bottom was a space for signature and date.

Each person was to sign both copies. Each participant stood, read the mission statement with their name inserted and turned in one copy of the certificate. The second was theirs to keep.

Later we framed a copy and created a Mission Wall of our own within the IT Department. It was incredibly powerful. As word spread throughout our company, many of our mission partners (fellow employees) came by to see the wall. Many expressed the desire to sign a certificate themselves.

The impact on the vendors can be best summed up by a phone call I received three years later from Larry Ferguson of CDW. He said, "Jeff, you know, I have that certificate hanging on the wall of my office and every time I look at it, I think of you guys and ask myself, how can I help you with the mission today."

PERFECT!

The Key - Continuous Improvement

The following year we made some adjustments to the summit to make it even better. We wanted to "break the ice" with our vendor partners prior to our discussion to improve the dialogue. To give the group time to get to know each other, we moved the formal dinner to the end of the first day, instead of the second. The vendor discussion would then be the following day. This would get the awkwardness out of the way.

This change meant we needed to change the location. We didn't want our vendor partners to have to drive to Nashville two days in a row or have to rent a hotel room. We moved to the Fort Harrison State Park Inn. It was a perfect venue.

We also asked the partners to prepare to present to us this year. We wanted them to talk about their specialties in the areas we purchased from them. The focus was to be on the trends they saw in that space, not "Hey, here is what we do."

The final change was the addition of an "adventure" as a part of the dinner. Only my Executive Assistant, Kay Haimes, and I knew of the adventure. The guests were instructed to dress casually.

Since we were at a State Park, we decided to take advantage of it. Our dinner was a cookout inside the park, complete with BBQ and corn on the cob. The surprise? Why a hayride, of course! So, yes, we took a group of about 30 technology sales professionals, some still dressed in suits, ties, dresses, and heels, on a hayride. The ice was indeed broken.

The next day, the discussion and dialogue was lively and filled with great insights for us to take away and incorporate into our annual revision of the strategic plan.

Partnerships Evolve

Year three, we continued to refine the process. The overall structure was the same: a day of meetings with my team, our vendor partners joining us for dinner, followed by a day two meeting with the vendors, wrapping up with the entire department joining for an afternoon discussion.

The biggest change was the inclusion of all the business unit heads on the first day. Rather than the IT team talking about the business plans, we wanted the business leaders themselves to present.

Oh, and the adventure? We conducted a Twitter scavenger hunt before the cookout. We met at a shelter house in the park and divided into teams with at least one vendor and one staff member. They were given clues of things to find throughout the park. They had to tweet a picture of their team at that location. First one back would win. We streamed the Twitter feed live at the shelter house. We kept the feed projected throughout the remainder of the evening.

Since we had focused the first year on Goodwill and the second year on the vendors and industry trends, we were now hitting our stride. Borrowing from a technique I had been using in our team meetings, we brainstormed the agenda live. With just my staff first, I wrote the word "agenda" on newsprint and asked, "OK, what do you want to talk about with our partners?" We came up with a list of about ten items. When the partners joined us, we repeated the process (but without letting them see our list). We then combined the lists. That became our discussion agenda.

If you've never tried this technique, let me tell you it's amazing to see the level of engagement. I'll give credit where credit it is due; it was my wife's idea after I had expressed frustration with having to, yet again, build a team meeting agenda.

Declaring Victory

The fourth year, we made a final revision to the summit. We were nearing the end of our five-year plan. In fact, we were about to declare victory on the goals of the original plan. Yes, we had been keeping the plan evergreen, but now was the time to author a new, bolder vision for the future. As we reviewed the list of our vendors, we divided the list into three types: transactional (lower spend, not a lot of interaction); key (high spend, still somewhat transactional), and strategic (forward thinkers, strong relationship).

We kept the same structure for the two days. Both our key vendors and strategic vendors were invited to the dinner at the end of day one. For the discussion on day two, we limited the invitation to the strategic vendors. Our discussion focused on the vision of the future. Three years from now, five years from now, what would technology look like? What would Goodwill look like? How would the changes in technology impact Goodwill's mission?

We also combined the adventure and the dinner into one big event. We threw a huge New Year's Eve Party, complete with a live DJ (thank you, Mr. Kinetik), even though it was July. What better way to mark the end of our initial five-year plan than the way it was launched? The night included a look back at what everyone in the room had accomplished in the last five years. It truly was a celebration.

The Results

What were the results of these annual efforts? Incredibly strong partnerships. We knew our business arrangements were fair and equitable for both parties. They knew our financial and resource constraints; we knew their margins and market challenges. We were able to tap into some of the best and brightest minds in technology AND in business. And I knew (because I experienced it time and time again) whatever I needed, no matter day or night, I could call, and they would be there, no questions asked, no discussion of Ts and Cs or SLAs. They would be there. They knew we would make it right in the end. They knew we were partners, in this together.

I believe you would be well served to develop a program similar to this. The relationships you build will pay significant dividends for your team and your organization. I also encourage you to keep the "adventure" element. It may seem hokey at first; however, I think it is an integral part to building these relationships. Those involved will talk about them for years, not just among each other but also with outsiders. Your reputation as a fair and equal partner will set you apart in the eyes of many.

The partners who attended our summits varied through the years. New partners were added, our relationships with others changed (such as with the partner who supported our SAN. Once you go cloud, you don't really need a SAN anymore), sometimes the relationship became more transactional. I know I will regret doing this, but I need to thank some of the companies that were our partners during this time. I say regret because I know I will forget someone.

Thank you for your support; thank you for your partnership! BD Managed Services, BKD, Bluelock, CDW, CIM Audio-Visual, Comcast, ESI, Hourly CIO, Inter-Vision (Bluelock Solutions) MCPc, Netfor, OneBridge (formerly SmartIT), Pondurance, Sensory Technologies,

Sinewave, TEK Systems, TW Telecom (now part of CenturyLink), and Van Ausdall & Farrar. This is not to be considered an endorsement of these firms by Goodwill. However, it is my personal endorsement of these firms, the staff that represented them, and the partnerships that were formed.

We've been speaking a lot about moving to the cloud, so, let's take a journey to the cloud. Several of the partners mentioned above were integral to our journey, but Hourly CIO made our first giant step an easy one!

10

TAKE A JOURNEY TO THE CLOUD

At a recent gathering of Chief Information Officers, the moderator asked by show of hands who had a cloud strategy. Two of 30 raised their hands. The moderator then asked how many had at least one application running in the cloud. All 30. What was going on here? How could so many companies be venturing into the cloud without a strategy of *why* or a plan of *how*? Do you *need* a cloud strategy? I say the answer is "Yes!"

I can hear some of the naysayers now. "You don't need a cloud strategy, or a digital strategy, or an IT strategy; what you need is a business strategy." I couldn't agree more. None of those things are about the technology; they are enablers of the business strategy. They should all help drive the business toward its goals. If you work for a company that has a clearly defined strategy, count yourself lucky. For the rest of you, your first step might be to help the company articulate its strategy. If you are unable to affect that shift, at the very least, you need to define the strategy, *as you understand it,* as a basis for any technology strategy.

Cloud First

Just as an IT strategy needs to be part of a broader business strategy, a cloud strategy is a part of an overall IT strategy. It should answer the question of "why" and "when" in business terms, not in technology terms. During the execution of our five-year plan, we took a very aggressive "cloud first" strategy as part of the overall corporate strategy.

For a 100-year-old company, we were very entrepreneurial. We wanted to be able to start new business ventures quickly. If they could provide jobs, provide revenue, or both, and they fit within our mission, we didn't want to wait months or years for IT to catch up. Therefore, our first "why" was agility.

To support those ventures, we needed to be able to ramp up quickly and without a long-term commitment. If the venture was not successful, we needed to be able to shut it down just as quickly and without a lingering financial burden. This led us to our second "why": elasticity, the ability to scale up and collapse down on demand.

Finally, we had to do all of that without adding new headcount into IT (similar to the second "why," this would add lingering financial burden). IT could not grow linearly with revenue and needed to show economies of scale. Our third "why" was "lean."

Cloud Strategy Statement

Had we written our cloud strategy in statement form, it would have looked like this:

To provide agility and elasticity in support of the ever-dynamic business environment and to maintain a lean IT team, when a new application is needed or a refactor of an existing application is called for, we will follow the order of:

- Software-as-a-Service (SaaS) offerings – if none found -
- Hosted applications offerings – if none found -
- On-Premises applications – if none found -
- Build it ourselves in a "Cloud Ready or Friendly" environment

We will examine our existing application portfolio and identify opportunities to leverage as-a-Service cloud offerings when and where appropriate to enable the IT team to focus on higher-value projects and tasks.

We estimate current time allocation is 80 percent Keeping the Lights On (KLO) and 20 percent New Functionality and Innovation. We believe by following this strategy, we will swing the allocation in favor of New and Innovation, therefore furthering the mission of the organization. In addition, we believe implementing this strategy will enable our fellow employees to have access to our IT assets anytime, any place, via any device, allowing them to perform their roles more efficiently and effectively.

The strategy then needs to tie back to the overall company strategic plan by referencing key points in that plan, identifying the impact to the Key Performance Indicators (KPIs) you will achieve (or in some cases defining new KPIs). As an example, if you are a retail company, you might say, "By focusing more on innovation, we will identify ways to increase store efficiency, improve the shopping experience and therefore drive revenue per customer visit up by 15 percent."

Impacts of a Cloud Strategy

There are two key areas a cloud strategy should also address, one obvious, and one not-so-obvious: security and vendor management.

From a security perspective, it is important to understand the business's overall stance on security (and compliance). What are the data the company values most? What personal information about its customers and employees does it retain? What applications contain this data? How does this data need to be secured? What compliance standards or regulations does the business need to achieve?

The answers to these questions should be addressed specifically in the strategy. How will they be addressed and what limitations do they put on the strategy? Just because a cloud vendor is storing your data does not relieve your company from the responsibility of protecting the data and meeting compliance standards or regulations.

For us, part of our IT strategy that flowed to our cloud strategy was the stance that we were not going to store customer credit cardholder information in any of our applications or let it traverse our network "in the clear" (unencrypted). That strategy statement led us to implement applications, processes and technologies in a much different manner than had been done in the past.

The second area of vendor management might come as a surprise to many, but it can play a significant role in the implementation of a cloud strategy. After all, cloud is really just a different form of outsourcing. Vendor management encompasses a lot of different aspects, many of which I will dive into in future chapters. I do want to mention two areas here. As with any relationship between two companies, the contractual agreement is critical. Agreements should be reviewed by counsel with experience in technology contracts and, more specifically, cloud technology contracts. Areas like service level agreements, data ownership, access during disputes, and liability and indemnification related to data breaches must all be spelled out clearly and fairly. You'd be surprised how many standard SaaS application agreements don't include these clauses.

The other aspect of vendor management that should be called out in your cloud strategy is "cultural fit." Because the company will be entrusting some of its critical applications and processes to a vendor partner, that partnership will be vital to success in many cases. The cloud strategy should call out when a cultural fit is important and to what degree. For example, there is little need to have a cultural fit with an email SaaS provider. Typically, there will be very little interaction with the provider. However, there will be significant interaction with a business intelligence SaaS, disaster recovery-as-a-service or infrastructure-as-a-service provider. Therefore, the level of cultural fit will be much more important.

Do you need a cloud strategy? My answer is an emphatic "Yes (as a part of your overall IT strategy, in support of your overall business strategy)!"

Our Journey to the Cloud Started with...Email

February 6, 2012, a historic date in Indianapolis, Indiana. Yeah, there was some little football game that night, Super Bowl XLVI – New York Giants against the New England Patriots. But that is not the event that made the date memorable for several of us. What made that date historic was our go-live on Google Apps, our first step in our journey to the cloud.

In 2010, we were running Microsoft Exchange 2003 coupled with Outlook 2010. Back in the day, the adage was "No one ever got fired for buying IBM." I was in the "No one ever got fired for buying Microsoft" camp. In fact, when I learned the students in our high school were using Google, I was pretty adamant that they use Office. After all, that is likely what they would be using when they entered the workforce.

At about this same time, we were switching from BlackBerry to Android-based smartphones. We were having horrible sync problems between Exchange and the Androids using ActiveSync. We needed to upgrade our Exchange environment desperately.

It was in this context the description of A-C versus C-F Projects echoed in my brain. Email upgrades are a horrible waste of resources. Managing email on a day-to-day basis is even more horrible. I could not fathom a more likely C-F project than an email upgrade project. Why not look to the cloud? Since we were doing an upgrade anyway, perhaps this would be the last email upgrade we would have to do.

The Google Whisperer

Enter the Google Whisperer. For months, a former colleague-turned-Google-consultant (doing business as Hourly CIO) had been telling me we should check out Google as an email platform. Usually my response was "Google? That's for kids, not an enterprise!" Every time I saw him, he would bring it up. I finally agreed to attend one of Google's roadshow presentations. I came away from that event with an entirely different outlook (pun intended) on Google.

We decided to run an A/B pilot. We would convert 30 employees to the Google Apps platform for 60 days. We would then convert the same 30 employees to BPOS (predecessor to Office 365) for 60 days and may the best man—er, platform—win. We handpicked the employees for the pilot. I purposely selected many who were staunchly in the Microsoft camp and several others who typically resisted change.

At the end of the pilot, an amazing thing happened. Not one person on the pilot team wanted to switch from Google to BPOS. In fact, each person voted to recommend a Google migration to the executive team. Unanimously! When was the last time that ever happened in one of your projects?!!?

Go and Get Your Google on!

The decision made, we launched the project to migrate to the cloud! One of the most challenging aspects of the project was the decision to use this as the impetus to implement an email retention policy. During the Process & Policy initiative of the strategic plan, the executive team had wrestled with and settled upon a five-year retention policy.

This meant tracking down all of the PST (Personal Storage Tables) people had created from Outlook over the years. The vast majority of the work in the project involved locating all these files on our network file stores, local hard drives, and, yes, even thumb drives and CDs. Once located, they were moved to a central location, and the original PST destroyed. Our consultant was then able to upload them to the Google platform.

During this time, we also mirrored our email environment so every internal and external email also went to the Google platform in real time. This enabled us to focus on uploading older emails before our official launch.

Game Time!

The process took about three months, but finally, it was Super Bowl Sunday, time for go-live. Now before you think me an ogre of a boss for scheduling a major go-live for Super Bowl Sunday, I should tell you, the project team selected the date of February 6, 2012. Their reasoning was that no one was going to be doing email after the game was over. We announced a blackout period of eight hours beginning at midnight to do our conversion.

Boy, were we ever wrong about the length of the blackout period. Our conversion that night took about 20 minutes. Only 20 minutes, and email was flowing again in and out of the Google environment. Monday morning our team arrived early to greet the employees as they entered, help them with any questions they had, and ensure their smartphones were connected to email where appropriate.

Our implementation included email, contacts, calendar, and groups for three domains. We made the decision to keep the other Google Apps available, but not promote them. We also implemented our five-year archive and optional email encryption for sensitive communications. The other decision we made (OK, *I* made) was not to allow the use of Outlook to access Gmail. One of the tenets of our strategic plan was "Any time, any place, any device." I felt having a piece of client software violated that tenet and created additional support issues that were not necessary.

A Hiccup and Some Lessons Learned

Meetings. The bane of business everywhere. Meetings, or at least the scheduling of conference rooms, turned out to be the bane of our conversion. More specifically, recurring meetings. We talked early about the pilot group using Google. As you might imagine, many of those employees booked conference rooms for meetings, some of them recurring. Others still on the legacy calendaring system were also scheduling meetings well into the future. We now had "claims" from two different systems for the same physical conference rooms, not to mention we found dozens of orphaned bookings (you know, the room reservation that can't be deleted for whatever reason?). The team decided our best bet was to release the conference rooms from conversion day forward. The IT team worked with the meeting organizers to re-book the conference rooms the morning after go-live. The team did a fantastic job, thus removing any excuse for missing a meeting!

We learned several things as a result of the project. First, search is not the same as sort. If you have used Gmail, then you know there is not a way to sort your Inbox; it relies instead on the power of Google Search. People *really* liked the sort function, and it took some handholding to get them comfortable with the new option.

Second, Google Groups are not Distribution Lists. We converted all of our Exchange Distribution Lists to Groups. Yes, they do function in somewhat the same way; however, there are many more settings in Groups, settings that can have unexpected consequences. Consequences like the time our CFO replied to an email that had been sent to a Group, and even though he did not use reply all, his reply went to everyone in the Group! We found that setting *very* quickly and turned it off. (Sorry, Dan!)

The third lesson learned was "You cannot train enough." Yes, we held many classes during the lead up to conversion and continued them long afterward. A lot of the feedback we had heard ("everyone has Gmail at home, we already know how to use it") led us to believe once the initial project was complete, we didn't need to continue training. We soon realized we need to resurrect the classes and started a series of Google Workshops to continue the learning process. Honestly, I think some of this is generational. Some love to click on links, watch a video, and then use the new functionality. Others really want a classroom environment. We began to offer both.

One of the things that pleasantly surprised us (well, at least me) was the organic adoption of other Google tools. The first shared Google Doc came to me from outside the IT Department. The first meeting conducted using Google Hangouts came from the Marketing Department. People were finding the apps and falling in love with them.

With our Cloud Strategy defined and our first major conversion under our belt, we turned our attention to other projects. If it was a C-F project, our focus was on finding an alternative delivery method. If it was an A-C project, our focus was on delivering the highest achievable value to the company.

REAP THE REWARDS

A mplify your value, and you can reap the rewards. That's kind of the theme of this entire book—how you can amplify the value of your IT department *and* how your company can reap the rewards. This chapter is not a summary of our journey. It is about our next step on the journey. It is a chapter about an organization that was moving headfirst into the cloud, moving headfirst into a "buy versus build" strategy, and moving headfirst into changing its operating model. It's a chapter about an organization that decided to develop its own loyalty card program and in the process executed one of the most impactful "IT projects" in the 85-year history of the company. But ... let me start at the beginning.

An Eight-Year Roadblock

It was mid 2010, and I had just joined Goodwill Industries of Central Indiana as CIO. That first week, one of the meetings I had—in fact, the first meeting with a peer VP—was with our VP of Marketing. That meeting covered a *lot* of ground and various topics. One that stood out for me was when she mentioned Goodwill had been discussing gift cards and loyalty cards for about eight or ten years, but it never seemed to move forward. She even pulled out a folder that had enough of a thud factor to make any contract attorney jealous. It contained page after page of meeting minutes, email correspondence, and requirements. I was floored...eight years? Of talking? What was the roadblock?

A few days later, I was meeting with the VP of Retail. Again, we talked about a lot of different topics. Sure enough, the conversation soon rolled around to gift cards and loyalty cards. We've been talking about it for eight years...and we've made no progress...eight years? Of talking? What was the roadblock?

That afternoon, I met with a couple of folks from my new staff. "What's up with this gift card and loyalty card thing?" I asked. Eight years? Of talking? What was the roadblock?

So, since this is my book, I get to use my soapbox to air some dirty laundry and perhaps, according to who you ask, some revisionist history. It seemed the problem was that Marketing blamed Retail's inability to define requirements; Retail blamed IT for always saying "No, we can't do that," and IT blamed Marketing for wanting to discuss ad nauseam but never move forward. I vowed that this would change. So, in the midst of our strategic planning process, I called a meeting to discuss gift cards and loyalty cards. After all, early in my career, I had spent 12 years in banking, specifically in credit cards.

Gift Cards were the Easy Part

As the year progressed, we began to define requirements and search commercial offerings for gift and loyalty cards. The project hadn't been in progress very long when the team decided to separate the project into two phases. Phase one would be gift cards, and phase two would be loyalty cards. With that decision, the project kicked into high gear. Given our Point of Sale system and our requirements, we very quickly identified a gift card software provider. Within a few short months, we launched our gift card program.

Several weeks later, we reconvened our team of Marketing, Retail and IT to start on loyalty cards. We further defined our requirements. We wanted a random reward system, not a points-based system. We wanted flexibility in the rewards offered, and, most importantly, we wanted to track and drive two different behaviors on the same card: shopping and donating. Throughout the winter, we evaluated many off-the-shelf solutions. However, it became readily apparent that no off-the-shelf solution was going to meet our requirements. Sure, they all offered flexibility in the rewards, but they were all based on earning points. None of them could track two different behaviors on the same card. Even taking that into consideration, the team was narrowing the selection down to a handful of packages that met at least some of the requirements.

A Dark Horse Enters the Race

I knew we had to build it. We had to deviate from our cloud-first buy strategy and build it ourselves. There was no other way. With that in mind, we developed our own response to the RFP we had issued. It was basically a general design document of what could be built. We submitted our "RFP Response" to the team along with the two or three commercial packages that had been down-selected. As selection day quickly approached, I made it a point to discuss the proposal in detail with the VP of Retail and the VP of Marketing. I could tell they were skeptical that IT could pull it off. I assured them we could, and quite frankly, played the "new guy" card and asked for a chance.

Our proposal was selected. Now it was time to put up or shut up. We engaged with a local firm (Arete Software) to build the initial database and prototype. Once we had a working prototype, we shifted to the internal team. As we worked feverishly on the code, the project team defined the goals and the targets for success. The launch date would be November 11, 2011 (11/11/11); we would achieve an 11 percent increase in retail sales; our average shopping cart would increase by $0.50, and we would have 100,000 cardholders at the end of the first year.

Over the course of the summer and the fall, the team worked faithfully to hit the target date. Finally...it went live. The organization that was moving headfirst into the cloud, moving headfirst into buy versus build, moving headfirst into changing its operating model, launched its loyalty card program: Goodwill Rewards™.

The Race was Won

Yes, we hit our target dates; yes, we hit our budget. But, how did we do on our business goals? Our increase in retail sales was 13 percent, beating our target by 2 percent; average shopping cart grew by $0.53, beating target by $.03, and we *blew* past the 100,000-cardholder mark in under six months. In fact, at the end of year one, we had over a quarter of a million cardholders. Within a couple of years, we had over 550,000 (remarkable, considering the geographic territory is 29 counties in Central Indiana. Yes, we gained over half a million cardholders in just 29 counties of Indiana).

To further validate our success, we were awarded the Society of Information Management of Indiana's Innovation of the Year award in 2012. Not only did we meet our business goals, but also our IT peers recognized the accomplishment.

How were we able to achieve this? First, it truly was a team effort. In fact, I believe one of the most important outcomes of this project was for Marketing, Retail and IT to work together *as a team,* to achieve a common goal. Second, our path to amplify our value by leveraging cloud technologies and avoiding C-F Projects enabled us to spend our energy on this A-C project. Third, the environment and culture enabled us to take a risk, to step into the unknown, to ask for and receive the support to move forward.

We had a multitude of lessons learned, of course. One of the biggest surrounded holiday sales. There are some holidays the stores are open, but foot traffic is very low. Our thought was to give the Reward members a surprise holiday reward to incent them to shop. It worked, sort of. Overall foot traffic increased substantially; the number of transactions increased dramatically; however, Year-over-Year sales were flat and at some stores went down. What happened?

The benefit of the new system was that we now had the data to answer that question. After analyzing, we realized the $5.00 off reward did incent shoppers, but the average shopping cart had dropped. Many shoppers bought items totaling $5 or $6, resulting in purchases of zero or $1. We quickly changed to the parameters on the holiday sales to require a minimum purchase of $20.

Revenue Generation

Another opportunity grew out of this success. Goodwill Industries International is actually made up of over 180 independent businesses that all share the same brand. Each is locally owned and operated and opts to join the broader membership. As we began to talk about the success of the loyalty card program across the membership, several of the agencies approached us about the possibility of licensing the software.

This was not something we had considered during the development of the system, but if the organization used the same Point-of-Sale system as we did, it should be fairly straightforward. After talking it over with the CEO and others, we agreed to package and license the software. It took a few weeks of work, along with the development of a license agreement and some on-site implementation support from our lead developer, and we were in receipt of our very first revenue check.

Because we knew our department had not been built to be a software publishing company, we developed an "as-is", no warranty, no support license agreement. The license fee was a one-time fee.

Over the course of the next several months, we discussed the possibility of developing this concept further and building an organization to surround the loyalty card software as a product offering. After investigating the business case, we decided the addressable market could not support the concept.

As an alternative, we explored the possibility of building a gated open source community. In other words, we would not put the software fully in the public domain, but instead, assess a nominal fee to any Goodwill organization in good standing to join the community. For the fee, they would have full access to the source code. In this way, the code could continue to be developed and forked, and all the members could take advantage of it. At the end of the day, we decided it would detract from the focus of driving our organization forward.

Even though we decided not to expand the availability, the revenue we did generate from selling a handful of the "as-is" licenses offset the some of the development costs of continuing to expand the functionality for our own use.

Core Principles

The Goodwill Rewards development project was a great example of using the core principles articulated during the strategic plan process to guide our process. We were a "buy shop." In the chapter on process improvement, we stated:

Principle	Amplification:
We purchase systems rather than custom-develop our own systems unless a quantified competitive advantage can be proven.	Competitive advantage in-cludes timing, migration cost, maintenance, support and entry barri-ers. Given our ERP foundation, we will seek software that interacts with the following systems, in the following order: • ERP Core Modules • Core Applications • Portal Applications • Software-as-a-Service Applications • Commercial off the shelf (COTS) • Custom Develop (Using our Standard Platform)

In this case, we exhausted all of the options described above. None of the first five solutions would have met the business need. We had to build it ourselves. In the next chapter, we will explore two examples in which the answer was to *change* a Core Principle, instead.

12

CORE PRINCIPLES PUT TO THE TEST

To ERP or not to ERP

In Chapter 6, we discussed adopting a set of core principles to help guide your team and provide context to others within your company. With the roll-out of a core ERP system just prior to starting our strategic planning process, we adopted the above as an Application Portfolio Core Principle. Within the first year, the principle was put to the test.

Principle	Amplification:
We seek Enterprise Resource Planning (ERP) solutions that are either part of the core ERP or that integrate well and provide uniform solutions across business units.	Given the Company business model, it is important to have a core system that can be leveraged across the various business units. To gain further efficiencies and standardized data, we will look first to the ERP functionality and where possible adjust business process to fit the core. Where this is not possible we will seek solutions that integrate well into the core and share common infrastructure.

A project to implement a Human Resource Information System (HRIS) was submitted to and approved by the executive team. As a part of that initial discussion, we reminded the group of the core principle. The implication was that the project team would look first at the HRIS that was a part of our ERP system. We needed to take a fair and objective look at the requirements and compare them to the HRIS module. There needed to be compelling reasons not to select and implement that module.

With that understanding, the project team was assembled. They spent several weeks developing their list of requirements. As they worked, it was becoming obvious the ERP module was going to fall woefully short. Almost all of the shortcomings were in business requirements rather than technical requirements. At the end of the evaluation, it was unanimous. The ERP module would not meet our needs, nor were there any integrated third-party packages available.

Does the Exception Prove the Rule or Does the Rule Change?

The executive team deliberated for a short time and made the decision to deviate from the core principle. As CIO, I then raised the question, "Is this an exception to the principle, or is this a change to the core principle?" *That* question took a bit more time to consider. We wrestled with the pros and cons. The business units leaders already on the ERP asked, "How does that impact us? Can we re-evaluate the selection of the ERP?" Those not yet on it argued they should not be restricted to only one choice.

After a couple weeks of discussion, we decided to change the core principle from ERP focused to Best-of-Breed focused. This was a healthy process. The decision to change was not taken lightly, and in the end, everyone was heard. This serves as a great example of the use of the core principles. First, it focused the project team right out of the gate. Had the ERP module fit the business requirements, we could have gone right into the planning phase for implementation. Exceptions to the core principles can be made, but they need to be made thoughtfully and at the right level of the organization. Second, the two discussions were excellent exercises for the executive team. We were wrestling with business strategy, not a technology decision.

Lessons Beyond an HRIS

This project also contained some other valuable lessons. After the decision to look outside of the ERP was made, the team gathered a list of viable HRIS products for selection. At the annual MIT CIO Symposium (if you don't attend, you should!), I had heard of an up-and-coming force to be reckoned with in the HRIS space: Workday, a born in the cloud, SaaS-based product. Upon returning from the conference, I put their name on the list to be considered.

Sensitive the perception of swaying the decision, I remained a neutral co-executive sponsor with the VP of HR. The team did an outstanding job of vetting the potential solutions and the companies representing those solutions. After several months, they had decided to move forward with a different product. They made a compelling case, and I supported their decision and recommendation.

However, circumstances had changed. Revenues for the year were not meeting expectations, so the project was shelved. Fast forward 18 months. We were enjoying better results, and the need to have an HRIS for a company now exceeding 3,000 employees was hard to put off any longer. We re-launched the project. Knowing many of the systems had multiple releases in the interim, I instructed the team to take six weeks and review the top three candidates again.

I was floored (pleasantly but floored just the same) when the team came back with the decision to go with Workday. It was, in fact, a unanimous recommendation from the team. The project itself was not without its bumps and bruises, but the CFO still considers it the best decision and most impactful implementation in his tenure (interesting to note, the financials were running on the ERP).

What had happened in the intervening months to change the decision? Of course, Workday had released new functionality, but had I put undue pressure on the team? Had I expressed too much disappointment with the initial choice? I believe Workday was maturing its product offering. But I believe it was also a sign of our maturing organization. The technology strategies we had implemented were truly supporting the business strategies and I believe our partners in the business were experiencing success because our alignment. Alignment builds trust.

First, we had defined our cloud strategy. Cloud was no longer a large unknown. We knew when we would use cloud (and in this case SaaS) to solve business problems and when we would not. In Chapter 11, we discussed the cloud strategy we had defined. Workday was cloud from the ground up. Many of their competitors had taken the on-premises version of their software and pushed it to a cloud but were missing a key component of SaaS-based cloud applications: single code base multitenancy.

Second, we had implemented several other SaaS applications, increasing the team's comfort factor. This included Efforts-to-Outcome for our mission-based tracking and report, Salesforce for our business development efforts, Wealth Engine to support our fundraising efforts, and Facility Dude to manage facility-related maintenance requests (and the product with the coolest name ever!).

Third, we had continued to articulate the vision, the vision of what could be as we implemented the strategic plan. The organization as a whole was beginning to see and understand. The results were speaking for themselves. IT had found its voice, and we were gaining credibility. We were moving further and further around the dial, edging much closer to becoming a value-add partner.

DOMO ARIGATO

Principle	Amplification:
Standard applications will be identified by major business processes. We will strive to move to those standards and only deviate where a quantifiable business advantage exists or when program requirements or funding dictates.	Multiple applications providing the same or very similar functionality increase costs and complexities of support. Selecting non-standard applications may require the use of external resources to support. The Company IT Standards Process will define the standards and the process by which standards can be amended.

I've mentioned "ride alongs" elsewhere in this book. Ride alongs are the practice of getting out of the office and accompanying one of the other executives as they go about their day. Typically, for us, this meant someone in retail. I found that I learned not only about our business and the executive but also about leadership and my own professional growth. I have no doubt we would not have been as successful on our strategic plan journey if not for these ride alongs.

It was during one of those ride alongs with Kent Kramer, Goodwill's Chief Operating Officer at the time (and now CEO), that he asked me, "Hey, have you ever heard of Domo?"

I countered immediately with, "Do you mean 'Domo Arigato,' that song by Styx?"

He glanced over at me with one of those, "Uh, no!" looks and retorted, "No, I mean Domo the BI tool."

Business Intelligence tool? I was surprised; aside from reporting, there had been no real appetite for true business intelligence tools. In fact, IT had tried to introduce the concept a year earlier, and it had fallen flat. There was no energy behind it. Maybe now was the time?

Kent went on to explain. As COO, he needed more visibility into the business units. He wanted each of the BUs to become data-driven organizations. He couldn't do it if he had to wait for IT to build reports. Besides, he said, columnar reports are not at all effective on mobile devices. He and his teams were on the road. The reports needed to be easy to interpret at a glance. Building new metrics needed to intuitive for managers and directors. And, above all, the tools need to be mobile. His team was on the road more than they were in the office.

Research Begins

In my mind I was building a solid requirements list for a project to identify, select, and implement a BI platform. I promised Kent I would take a look at Domo but reminded him we already had a BI tool in use in the education division. I took the token to set up a demo of that solution for Kent and his team.

Never having heard of Domo, I started with research and soon learned it was a born-in-the-cloud business intelligence and data visualization tool. I ran through the online demo and found it to be robust, but what online demo doesn't make its product look good? I was still a bit skeptical. One of our core principles is "we run standard software." Since the education division had already selected a BI tool, there would need to be a compelling reason to support more than one.

I will say, Domo's digital marketing was pure genius. After watching the demo, their ads showed up EVERY-WHERE—LinkedIn, Facebook, news sites. No chance I was going to forget the name of the product.

To Kent's credit, he and his team spent a couple of hours at a hands-on demo of the product the education division was using. To say they were underwhelmed would be an understatement. And they were right. It wasn't very easy to understand, nor was it easy to use. In addition, it was an on-premises solution and required substantial support from IT resources, including an external partner.

Still, was that compelling enough?

We scheduled a live demo of Domo (demo of Domo—say that 10 times fast). It blew everyone away.

Still, was that compelling enough?

Kent and I packed our bags and headed out to the Gartner Data & Analytics Conference. We spent several days previewing hundreds of products, yet we kept coming back to Domo.

Kent put together a business case, and we took it to the executive team. As it turned out, the business case was compelling enough. The team decided to grant a variance to the core principle and fund a project to implement Domo. When I asked if this necessitated a change in the principle, the answer was a quick and decisive "no." Everyone agreed a discussion like we'd had was necessary and that deviating from standard should not be taken lightly.

These examples underscore the value of having the core principles in place and the process used to confirm, vary, or change them. The process ensures all parties are thinking of the best interests of the organization as a whole and taking all available information into consideration when rendering a decision. They were driving the right discussions at the right level of the organization.

Now it was time to address one of the biggest C-F projects IT departments face (or ignore in many cases), Disaster Recovery. Treated as an insurance policy by most companies, Goodwill had taken it seriously and invested heavily. But I am getting ahead of myself.

13

A TALE OF TWO RECOVERIES

Monday, January 6, 2014: Not since the blizzard of '78 had a day started in this way. After receiving close to 18" of snow on Sunday, temperatures plunged, with wind chills of 40 and 50 below zero. My phone rang early that morning. It was our CEO. We needed to have an executive conference call. The mayor had declared a travel ban. We needed to shut down all of our locations (more than 80 locations). We needed to let employees know. Very quickly, we initiated our communication plan.

Within minutes of settling in on the couch to watch more of the morning news coverage of the Blizzard of '14, my phone rang again. This time it was our Senior Director of IT Operations. His words sent a chill down my spine, even though I was warm and cozy inside. "There is a major power outage in downtown Indianapolis. Our headquarters is without power. All of our servers have shut down. We are dead in the water."

"Well, at least we are closed today," I thought.

"The power company says it will be 48 hours or longer until we have power. The team is on a Google Hangout right now discussing options."

I jumped on the Hangout and got a quick recap of the situation. Everything at corporate was down (including our server room). UPS batteries were depleted, and the servers had shut down. The power company estimated it would be 48 to 72 hours before power was restored. We had three options 1) declare a disaster and begin recovery to our warm site on the west side 2) rent a generator, have it delivered and installed, and power the server room 3) wait. Knowing our history of disaster recovery testing, I advised the team to explore the feasibility of option two while I instituted phase I of our Business Continuity Plan by sending notice to the executive team and firing up a conference bridge (the executives weren't quite Google Hangout savvy).

With the Hangout still live in my home office, I explained the status to our CEO, COO, and CFO. A disaster recovery would realistically take 24 hours, AND it was one-directional. Once live at the warm site, it would take weeks or months of planning to "come back" to corporate. The generator option was a possibility, but we didn't know yet. Or, we wait. The line was silent. None of those options were appealing. I quickly pointed out the good news: email was still working! (My boss, the CEO, loved it when I pointed out the obvious, especially when it underscored what a great decision it was to move to Google and the cloud. It's kind of like telling your spouse "I told you so"! It goes over VERY well.)

Putting the conference bridge on hold, I jumped back to the Hangout just in time to hear someone ask, "Did anyone check the power at the warm site?" GREAT question since our warm site was eight miles due west of headquarters, and the storm had rolled in from the west. I could hear the click, click, click, click of someone checking the status. "Scratch option one. Warm site is dead, too."

With that, I went back to the conference bridge. Since doing nothing seemed like a CLM (career limiting move), I informed them the warm site was down and that we were executing option two.

A Different Story

Fast forward to July. It was now about 130 degrees warmer. We were hosting visitors from another Goodwill organization in our boardroom. Down the hall, we were conducting a Disaster Recovery Test with our Mission Partners.

Let me repeat that in case you missed it. The CIO was sitting in a conference room talking with three or four executives from another Goodwill organization while his team was conducting a disaster recovery test, complete with Mission Partner testing.

The Back Story

OK, if you are still not seeing the nuance, let me give you some background. In 2009, we went live with our Business Continuity and Disaster Recovery Plan, including our warm site. Our investment was about nine months work and $500,000. That fall, we conducted a Recovery Test. Our users (because we called them that then) all gathered at the warm site to test their systems. Everything passed.

In 2010, we had a new CIO (me), a new systems engineer, and a couple of other new staff members. It was closing in on time to do our annual Business Continuity Test (including a mock scenario). Our systems engineer reviewed the documentation, spent some time at the warm site and then came into my office. "I don't know how they did it. They had to fake it! It had to be smoke and mirrors. There is no WAY they recovered the systems! I need two months to prepare."

GREAT. With a new CIO and a successful test last year, we needed two months to prepare this year. That was going to go over well. Guess I would have to use another punch on the "new guy" card. Two months later, we conducted another successful test.

October 2011, time for another test. I called the engineer into my office. "Are we ready?" I asked.

"Well, we've made some changes to the environment that have not been replicated to the DR site. You see, we've been busy. I need a couple months to get ready."

With steam coming out of my ears, I let him know we needed to be ready; we needed to document, and we needed to keep the environments in sync (shame on me; I thought we were doing all of that!).

A couple months later, we conducted the test. While it was declared successful, there were some bumps. At our lessons learned meeting, the team was … well, they were whining about not having enough time. After listening, I asked, "If we had a disaster today, would we be ready?" Again, after several minutes of this and that, I asked, "If we had a disaster today, would we be ready?" After about a minute of this and that, I interrupted, "I am declaring a disaster. This is a test and only a test. However, we are implementing our recovery NOW!"

After looking at me for several minutes and then realizing I was serious, the team headed out to the warm site to recover our systems again.

It was now fall of 2012. I was sick of the words "Disaster Recovery Test," yet it was that time again. We had a new systems engineer, the prior one having left earlier in the year. I stopped by his desk to ask about our preparedness for our disaster recovery test. "I've been looking at it. I don't know how it has ever worked. They must have faked it. It had to be smoke and mirrors. I need two months." Given he was now the new guy, I let him punch his card and gave him the two months. The test was successful.

Now do you see it? The CIO was sitting in a conference room talking with three or four executives from another Goodwill organization while his team was conducting a disaster recovery test, complete with Mission Partner testing. After *that* history? How could DR testing be a non-event?

DR Silver Bullet?

It started early in 2013. I was in my office with John Qualls of Bluelock and Steve Bullington of TWTelecom (now Centurylink). They were describing to me a new product and service from Bluelock and a partnership with TWTelecom. Bluelock was touting RaaS, or DRaaS, if you will. Disaster Recovery as a Service paired with TWTelecom's new Dynamic Capacity bandwidth. What?!!? You mean I can get rid of the warm site? Replace it with the elastic capacity of DR in the cloud? Combined with a team of professionals to manage it all? Leveraging bandwidth that can be dynamic based on our needs? All for less than I was spending today to depreciate the warm site investment? No more smoke, no mirrors? No more two months to prepare? Seemed like a no-brainer! Where do I sign up?

As luck would have it, our initial investment would be fully depreciated in the 3rd quarter of 2013. We were faced with a forklift upgrade to replace our servers and SAN at the warm site. The ROI was overwhelming. Due to competing priorities, we slated this project to start in mid-December so it would be complete by early in 2014. (If only I had a crystal ball!)

The project itself was pretty straightforward: establish the connectivity between the sites, install the Zerto agents on our servers, replicate the data and test! Easy peasy! We did experience some challenges (shocked to hear that, aren't you?). The biggest challenges were the visibility into our own environment, the initial seeding of the replication, and design hangover.

The Challenges

The visibility issue really could be summed up as "we didn't know what we didn't know" about our own environment. Over time, there had been a lot of cooks in the kitchen. We had a lot of servers whose function we weren't quite sure of. That, combined with terabytes of data that we weren't sure of either, led us to a lot of research to straighten the spaghetti (see how I did that? cooks in the kitchen...straighten the spaghetti...oh, never mind, back to the story).

The next challenge was the initial seed. Even though we knew the amount of data that had to replicate, and we sized the pipe accordingly, it was still taking an inordinate amount of time to create the first replication. Leveraging the Dynamic Capacity feature, we tripled the size of the pipe. It still took longer than anticipated; our own infrastructure became the limiting factor.

The final challenge, the one I like to call "design hangover," was all about how to provide an environment to our Mission Partners in which they could adequately test their applications. After whiteboarding option after option, none of which really provided a great answer, I asked a couple of questions. "So, it sounds like we are jumping through huge hoops to give a window to our Mission Partners. What happens in a real disaster? Do we have to go through all this?"

Our senior engineer explained, "No, because prod won't exist. You don't have to worry about duplicate addressing; you don't have to worry about changing IPs. You just see the recovered data. Look, I can show you right now. I can log into our portal at Bluelock and show you our data from my laptop."

"So?" I asked, slowly drawing out the sooooo, "We are going through all this so our Mission Partners can go to the business continuity site and test their applications? If it were a real disaster, they could go to the site and see their applications, no problem? What if we just let them come to this conference room, access their applications through your laptop and test? Would that be a valid test?"

"Well, yeah ... we thought they had to test from the BC site," the engineer responded hesitantly. (Translated that means "because we always did it that way"). I offered to raise it with the rest of the executive team, but I thought they would much rather have their teams walk down the hall to a conference room to test than drive across town and test.

Sure enough, they were all for it!

The Results

If only we had been done before the blizzard of 2014. Our results were phenomenal. First, we had true network segregation between our DR environment and production. Second, our Recovery Time Objective (RTO) was *under two hours!* (Disclaimer: our SLA was actually four hours on some servers and eight hours on others, but the whole thing finished in under two hours. One hundred VMs; 15 tbs of data) Third, our Recovery Point Objective was *THIRTY SECONDS!* Yes, an RTO of two hours and an RPO of 30 seconds loss of data. Fourth, our system architect and our system admin did absolutely nothing. Our CFO called Bluelock, gave them his code and hung up the phone. Two hours later, our System Architect's phone rang. "Your recovery instance is ready to test." BOOM! That's it! I've been around long enough to know there is no such thing as a silver bullet in IT, but this was pretty damn close.

Oh, and one more benefit? The response time of the applications during the test, using our recovered instance sitting in Las Vegas, was even faster than the response time of production sitting 30 feet away in our server room.

Another CF Project off the books. We now spend longer dreaming up the scenario for the re-enactment than we do preparing for and executing the DR test. So what have our system architect and system admin done with their extra time? How about spending time in Retail to understand the business needs and designing solutions for a queuing system to speed up the checkout lines, or designing the in-store digital displays for mission messaging throughout the store, or redesigning the power delivery to the POS systems providing extra run-time for less money, or designing SIP trunking for our VOIP system to provide call tree capabilities...or...or...

And what of that Blizzard of '14? We were lucky. Power was restored shortly after noon on the first day (thank you, Indianapolis Power & Light!), before the generator was even connected. We dodged *that* bullet, and now we are armed with a silver bullet.

We had a couple of more steps on our journey.

14

JUST ANOTHER SPOKE ON THE WHEEL

One of the most dramatic steps we took to becoming a value-add, revenue-generating partner
within the company was to completely throw
out our existing network. As I write that, it sounds a little
extreme. Let me explain.

Our network tied together over 70 locations in Central Indiana. A year or so before we embarked on our
five-year plan, we had implemented an MPLS network.
Most of the 70 locations were connected with T1s.

Our corporate headquarters housed our servers, storage, and the headend of our network. Out of that same

building, not only did we have corporate operations, but we also ran two charter high schools.

More Capacity

While this was a solid network providing four 9s of uptime, we were limited. Already our Loss Prevention Department wanted to view hi-def video from the stores, but over an 1.5 Mbps pipe viewing those video streams would bring the network to its knees. We certainly couldn't let them view one store's video from another store. So they were locked out from doing so.

We were already streaming music to the stores over the T1; however, we wanted to be able to push a video stream to our TV walls (the area where TVs for sale were displayed). We were sure we would sell more TVs if shoppers could see them in action. Again, we were stymied by the network bandwidth, so we put a DVD player in each store and mailed them a DVD every month.

Forget doing sales floor digital signage. No way was that going through a 1.5 Mbps needle.

Finally, even though we were on an MPLS network, we were essentially a hub and spoke network, with all of the traffic coming back to corporate before going out to the internet or to another location. If we were going to achieve our vision, if we were going to achieve our company's vision, we had to find a better way.

Can We Talk...

Our first step was to sit down with our telecom provider, TW Telecom (now Centurylink), and put our cards on the table. We could put in bigger pipes, but even the

T1s were several hundred dollars a month. How could we afford to put 10 or even 20 Mbps pipes in? Believe it or not, the plan we came up with would dramatically reduce their monthly recurring revenue (MRR), but we all agreed it was the right thing to meet our needs. We embarked on Phase I of our network redesign.

Phase I - Cable

Over the course of the next two years, we converted all of our retail locations to business-class cable. I can hear you now: "But what about quality of service? You don't get that with cable!??!" True. But to ensure we had the resiliency we needed, we put Verizon 4G in each store as our failover. In a very real sense, we multiplied our bandwidth over 10-fold, and added a backup circuit, both for 80 percent LESS a month than the cost of a T1. For our larger sites (e.g. schools, nursing, etc.), we put in larger point-to-point ethernet pipes (when possible fiber-based), with business-class cable as the failover.

The project was drawn out over two years for a variety of reasons. Primarily, we wanted to time the retirement of each of the existing connections with its renewal. However, we also ran into issues with getting right of entry from some of the landlords where our stores resided. We also had one store that was adjacent to a major highway construction project, which made it impossible for us to get cable service to the location. When we had finished moving all the other locations, we punted and put in a 10 Mbps point-to-point in that location. The plan was to revisit that store a few years later, when the highway was complete.

Phase II - Moving the Headend

As we were nearing the end of Phase I, we kicked off Phase II with the help of our networking partner, Sinewave. Phase II was to move the headend of our network out of corporate and into a state-of-the-art, fully compliant, fully certified data center. We chose Lifeline Data Centers. Specifically, we chose their eastside location. The data center was built in the old Eastgate Consumer Mall. This mall, long abandoned, had been built as an emergency bomb shelter during the cold war. Remember the Super Bowl that was held in Indianapolis? Homeland Security used the same data center for their command center.

The initial step was to swing all of our connections to Lifeline and land on Sinewave's hardware stack. This would enable us to reuse some of our existing gear to build out our new fully redundant stack. Once all of the traffic was successfully running through Lifeline, we swung it to run through our own gear.

As you might imagine, there were some complications with the migration. However, we were quickly able to resolve the issues as they cropped up (with a lot of help from Sinewave). Actual downtime to the stores and schools was minimal. Most of the issues we encountered caused excessive latency in some locations. Once we identified the offending traffic and changed its routing, response times returned to pre-migration levels.

Setting a New Standard

Once the network redesign was complete, we were able to help develop our new prototype retail store, complete with two 90"+ flat panels streaming hi-def content,

TV wall content that can now be centrally managed, SIP trunking to the stores to improve the phone systems, and a "Best-Buy-esque" queuing system to speed checkout.

We had one final step in our transformation.

The Final Step

The final step on our journey to amplify our value was also the most uneventful: we moved all of our production, test, and development environments to the cloud.

What?!!? You moved your entire data center to the cloud, and it was uneventful?

Yep, uneventful. In fact, on the night of January 10, 2015, the night we moved 75 servers, over 200 applications, several thousand device addresses and 15 terabytes of data, I, the CIO, was home in bed sound asleep.

Now, before you accuse me of being derelict in my duties as CIO, let me explain the level of confidence I had in the execution of this final step. As you have seen, it had been a five-year journey to amplify our value thus far. Our team was hitting on all cylinders. Our senior architect was (is) a rock star. He is one of those gifted individuals who can see the big picture AND all the minute details. I was confident he and our systems admin had it covered.

I was also confident in our partner in this endeavor. We had now been a client of Bluelock for a couple of years. I knew the level of talent they brought to the project as well. Every one of them was the top in his/her area. Confidence.

Earlier Steps Pay Off

One of the essential steps we had taken along our path to amplify our value also added to my confidence. In the chapter "A Tale of Two Recoveries," I told the story of our move to Bluelock for disaster recovery. This not only made the decision to trust them with our production environment an easy one, but it made the transport of all of our applications and data "easy" (remember I WAS home asleep) as well. You see, they already had all of our data and applications in their Las Vegas data center. Moving production was a matter of pointing the replication from one site to the other.

With all those moving parts, we only had two issues. One was with an outdated building automation system that had a hard-coded IP address, and the other was a typo on another IP address. Both of these issues were identified quickly and resolved. Though I will say, the result of the hard-coded IP address meant the building automation system left the HVAC system set to "unoccupied," which meant the headquarters building was 62 degrees. We decided to close the two schools in the building and send the kids home. (Kids, I am still waiting on the thank you...when I was in school, I had to walk two miles to school, uphill in both directions...never mind.)

The end result was that our headquarters truly was just another spoke on our hub and spoke topology network. The server room now only contained the switches and routers required to connect the employees there with their applications and the internet. Now a power outage like we had experienced the year before would be a non-event. The stores could still sell merchandise; the schools could still teach our children and adult students; the nursing program could still help first-time expectant mothers give birth to healthier babies; the manufacturing facility could still meet the needs of their customers, and all of our other mission-based programs could still help their clients.

Confidence. That sounds so much better than "It was so uneventful, it put me to sleep!"

THE DIAL REVISITED

This final step completed our journey to amplify our value. I've written elsewhere about the tremendous accomplishments this team achieved, so I won't repeat all of them. Here are just a few highlights:

- Opened 20 new retail stores
- Developed and launched a loyalty card program with now more than 500,000 customers
- Added 500 new jobs to the Central Indiana area
- Grew from one high school to 12, with more than 3,500 students and 1,900 graduates
- 26 new B2B customers
- 150 former inmates served by our New Beginnings program
- Over 800 babies born to first-time mothers through the Nurse-Family Partnerships program
- Fully automated our online auction processing, growing it to a $10 million business
- Implemented BYOD for smartphones
- Partnered with Netfor to provide a 24x7 service desk

- Dozens of new SaaS-delivered applications including: Workday, Domo, Facility Dude, Wealth Engine, Salesforce Marketing Cloud, and Director's Desk.

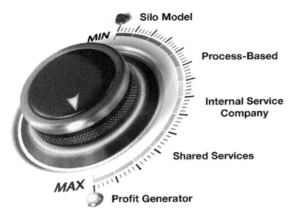

IT Business Models

Over the five-year period, we successfully moved from a reactionary Silo Model, through the steps of a Process-Based, Internal Service Company, Shared Services and finally to a value-add partner helping to drive top line revenue.

It began with an assessment based on proven standards and best practices. This assessment can be performed by a third party, or self-administered. If you've been at your company for more than a few months, I highly recommend utilizing a third party. You may have already developed blind spots that a third party can reveal. Reviewing the results of this assessment will give you an excellent understanding of your starting point.

From there, you can create a vision for the future. Identify the things you want to achieve. Paint a picture that tells the story. If you struggle to conceptualize the destination, invite a couple of creatives to join the discussion. As you and your team describe what it is you are trying to achieve, they will be able to help you find the images that tell your story.

Map out the major steps you will have to achieve to get from where you are today to where you want to be. Some of these steps will be obvious; some will reveal themselves over time. Prioritize the steps. Communicate the plan to your stakeholders using their language and imagery for maximum effectiveness.

Once you have buy-in, you can begin execution of the plan. Of course, you will have already started on some of the high-priority, high-value, low-cost parts of your journey. Make it a point to review your plan and your strategy at least once a year. Know when to stay the course and when to adjust the plan (and possibly the strategy) based on the changing environment.

Enjoy the journey!

ENDNOTES

"COBIT 5: A Business Framework for the Governance and Management of Enterprise IT." *COBIT Helps Organizations Meet Performance and Compliance Requirements*, www.isaca.org/cobit/pages/default.aspx.

"CMMI®." *CMMI Institute - CMMI Development*, www.cmmiinstitute.com/cmmi

"ITIL® - IT Service Management." *Axelos Corporate Site*, www.axelos.com/best-practice-solutions/itil

Ross, Jeanne W., et al. *Enterprise Architecture as Strategy: Creating a Foundation for Business Execution*. Harvard Business School Press.

REFERENCES

The following lists the companies we partnered with to achieve the transformations described in this book. These companies provide a breadth of services. I have chosen to indicate the services we used.

Mention of these organizations should not be considered an endorsement of them by Goodwill Industries of Central & Southern Indiana or Lauth Group, Inc. They have, however, my personal and professional endorsement.

Arete Software, Inc. http://aretesoftware.net/
Built the prototype for the application that would become Goodwill Rewards (™)

BD Managed Services,
http://www.bdmanagedservices.com
Structured Cabling

BKD, http://www.bkd.com/
ERP Support

Bluelock (InterVision), http://www.bluelock.com
Disaster Recovery as a Service, Infrastructure as a Service

CDW, https://www.cdw.com/
Infrastructure Hardware and Software

CIM Audio-Visual (CCS), https://ccsavpro.com/
Audio Visual equipment for the schools

Comcast Business, https://business.comcast.com/
  Data transport between locations

Domo, https://www.domo.com/
  Business Intelligence, Business Optimization

Electronic Strategies, Inc.
http://www.esitechadvisors.com
  SAN Hardware and Support

Hourly CIO, https://www.linkedin.com/in/bretthayes/
  Google Implementation and Support

Lifeline Data Centers, https://lifelinedatacenters.com/
  Co-location services for the headend of the network

MCPc, https://www.mcpc.com/
  Desktop and laptop procurement, configuration and
  deployment

Netfor, https://www.netfor.com/
  IT Service Desk, Desktop Deployment, Consumer
  Support Call Center, Home Pickup Scheduling

OneBridge, https://onebridge.tech/
  IT Staffing

Pondurance, https://www.pondurance.com/
  Cyber security, PCI DSS Assessment, Incident Response and Forensics

Resources Global Professionals, http://www.rgp.com/
  IT Assessments and audits

Sensory Technologies, https://sensorytechnologies.com
Audio-visual equipment and support for retail and corporate locations

Sinewave Technologies, http://sinewavetech.com/
Networking design, implementation, management and support

TEKsystems, https://www.teksystems.com/en
IT Staffing

TWTelecom (CenturyLink), http://www.level3.com/en/
Wide Area Network, MPLS Network, Internet

Van Ausdall & Farrar, https://www.vanausdall.com/
Printers and copiers procurement, leasing and support

Workday, https://www.workday.com/en-us/homepage.html
SaaS-based Human Resources Information System

RESOURCES

Electronic Versions of these resources are available at
www.JeffreyTon.com/AmpilyYourValue/Resources

Amplify Your Value - Strategic Plan Framework Outline

I. Executive Summary

This section appears first, but it is written last. After you have completed your strategic plan, write a summary of the key points you want the reader to take away. This section will only be a page or two. A great way of developing the executive summary is to think to yourself, "I have five minutes to make my pitch." In fact, I suggest reading it aloud when you are done. If it takes longer than five minutes, it's too long.

II. Introduction

This section is perhaps the most important. In the introduction you paint the picture; you create the image. The image must be vivid enough to catch the attention of the reader. As you paint the picture, you also answer the "why" and the "how." "Why" is your vision. Why do you do what you do? Why is it important to your business?

"How" is your bundle of strategies. How are you going to achieve your vision? Which strategies will keep you on the path? Speak to the decision makers in the language that resonates with them. You will need their support so you can execute the "what." What specific things are you going to do within the strategies to obtain your vision?

III. Current State Assessment

Think of this section as an executive summary of the department assessment you performed before launching the strategic planning process. Pull out the salient points from the assessment. Remember, you are still painting a picture. This section helps to support the "why." Allow the reader to "see" the impacts of status quo.

It is important to cover the current state of the market in which the business operates, the business itself, technology and the technology currently leveraged by the business, as well as the department resources and structure.

IV. Trends

A. Business Trends

B. Technology Trends

In the Current State section, you included some of the context in which the IT department operates, including your business, its industry, market and clients, and current technology. In this section, you describe the trends in each of those areas. How will your business change during the lifespan of the strategic plan? How will its clients' expectations change? How will technology evolve to meet those changes? AND how can you leverage that evolution to create a competitive advantage for your company?

V. Enterprise Architecture

In the Lauth strategic plan, we called these the "Elevations." In the world of commercial real estate, these are the drawings of the building being contemplated. For the purpose of your plan, this is where you describe the business's operating model and reveal (and explain) your core diagram.

When presenting or discussing your plan, collective understanding of this section will be paramount to the success of your plan. Take the time now to ensure everyone understands the Operating Model and Core Diagram. If needed, make changes based on the feedback you receive to make them even clearer.

VI. Organization

Undoubtedly, there will be impacts to your organization. Describe the current organization and then explain the envisioned organization. Detail the steps to migrate from one structure to the other.

VII. Vision, Mission, Governance and Core Principles

A. Vision

B. Mission

C. Governance

D. Core Principles

1. Application Portfolio Core Principles
2. Technology Infrastructure Core Principles
3. Investment Core Principles
4. Organization Core Principles

Define your department's mission and vision. This relates back to the "what." What do you want the IT department to become, and how does that vision relate to the corporate vision? The mission is the "how." How will IT partner with the other departments to deliver on the departmental vision and more importantly the corporate vision?

Lay out your governance structure. How will technology decisions be made? Who makes them? Is there a steering team? How will it operate?

Core principles are the guardrails. They help you and your team make decisions in the "heat of the battle." They are agreed upon through the governance structure. Any deviation from the core principles must be comprehensively thought through and vetted. These deviations should be wrestled with through the governance structure as well.

VIII. Recent Improvements

A. Process Improvement

B. Infrastructure Stabilization

C. R&D

D. Focus Topics

E. License Audits

You haven't been standing still while you've been developing your strategic plan, right? Here is where you let the world know all the great things you have already accomplished! Many times, these are process improvements, but they can also be projects that have been completed. Any work done to stabilize the systems and network should be called out here as well.

Brag. Part of running an IT department strategically is marketing the department to the rest of the organization. Celebrate your successes. Think of it like issuing a press release for each completed project.

IX. Roadmap

A. Short-Term Horizon

B. Mid-Term Horizon

C. Long-Term Horizon

This is the meat of the plan. Here, you lay out the projects and initiatives you need to complete to take you from point A to point B. The roadmap should be divided into short-term (under a year), mid-term (1-2 years) and long-term (beyond two years). The further out you go, the less concrete these ideas will be. In keeping with the image you created in your introduction, consider naming the projects within the same theme. For example, at Lauth, we labeled the three time horizons as: Delivery, Development and Pursuit. Some of the project names included Conduit, Cornerstone and Yellow Brick Road

(OK, that name might have been a bit of a stretch, but it sure paints a picture).

X. Budget

A.K.A "The Ask." You are going to need funding to implement all the wonderful things you have described. By now, you have them ready to be hooked. You've defined your vision, you've laid out your strategies, and you've shown them how you intend to realize the vision. Now it's time to show the costs. Your company undoubtedly has a format they are comfortable with when discussing budgets. Use it! Show them the variance. If there are savings in some areas, claim them. If there are investments necessary, explain them.

XI. Benchmarks

You either love 'em or you hate 'em. I've worked in organizations that lived and died by them (literally). I've worked in others that felt they were meaningless. Understand your culture before you include them (or not). If you do include them, make sure you are comparing apples to apples and oranges to oranges. Include corporate performance metrics. In other words, part of your message throughout your plan is "We are not average; we are outstanding." So be sure to compare against the leaders in your space, not the average.

XII. Conclusion

This is your close, your final pitch, your "ask." Here you tie it all together. To use the parlance of public speaking: in the Introduction you "tell 'em what you are going to tell 'em," then "you tell 'em," finally, in the conclusion, you "tell 'em what you told 'em." Make it a strong finish!

Amplify Your Value - Sample Core Principles

Electronic Versions of these resources are available at www.JeffreyTon.com/AmpilyYourValue/Resources.

Application Portfolio Core Principles

Principle	Amplification
We seek Enterprise Resource Planning (ERP) solutions that are either part of the core ERP or that integrate well and provide uniform solutions across business units.	Given the Company business model, it is important to have a core system that can be leveraged across the various business units. To gain further efficiencies and standardized data we will look first to the ERP functionality and where possible adjust business process to fit the core. Where this is not possible we will seek solutions that integrate well into the core and share common infrastructure.

171

Standard applications will be identified by major business processes. We will strive to move to those standards and only deviate where a quantifiable business advantage exists or when program requirements or funding dictates.	Multiple applications providing the same or very similar functionality increase costs and complexities of support. Selecting non-standard applications may require the use of external resources to support. The Company IT Standards Process will define the standards and the process by which standards can be amended.
We select solutions that integrate well within the overall architecture of Company.	Solutions should integrate to pass related data between applications rather than stand-alone point solutions. This reduces the requirement to key the same data in multiple times, improving productivity and increasing accuracy.
We maintain package integrity to accept new releases	Modifications to any application will be done in a controlled and specific manner. Forward compatibility will be given higher priority over business functionality. We do not want to be 'stuck' on an old release of an application that may prevent us from utilizing newer functionality.

We seek to standardize development platforms, languages, and toolsets and use a common methodology.	Deviation will only be done with the utmost consideration and evaluation. This will help us to control the costs associated with managing these assets. The Company IT Standards Process will define the standards and the process by which standards can be amended.
We value velocity and business impact more than functional elegance.	We need to be known for value delivery and speed, not for "perfect" software. Company's business moves too fast to be hampered by long project delays.
We implement leading-edge applications and upgrades with significant business value and prudent risk management.	Leading edge is great, but we must ensure value is verifiable and can be realized as we manage the prudent risks we take.
We plan and manage upgrades to our software using release management and configuration management.	This will enable us to maintain a stable production environment.

We avoid products that are not commercially supported. This includes ensuring we are on versions of commercial products that are maintained by the vendor.	Non-supported products put a tremendous drain on sustaining resources, driving up our costs for little or no benefit. The Company IT Refresh Process describes the release levels we will strive to maintain.
New Applications added to the portfolio must be accessible through Company's distributed network.	In order to operate within Company's distributed environment, it is essential for an application to run in a distributed manner. Therefore, applications will be required to be either: • Browser Based • WAN Certified in that order of preference.

Technology Infrastructure Core Principles

Principle	Amplification
We lead Company in the design of, and decision-making for, information technology wherever it is employed.	This includes Hardware, Systems software and Application software, Network, Telephony, Database and Platform.
We will manage the use of non-Company-owned devices for performing Company business by protecting and controlling the Company information and by protecting the Company Network	Supporting personal computing devices such as laptops, cell phones, printers and other such items can be extremely expensive and can present a risk to the Company computing systems. The Company IT Standards Process will define the standard equipment and the process by which the standard can be amended. With the advent of PDA's, smartphones, and other personal computing devices, rather than restrict their use, we will focus on data and network protection while providing limited support of these devices.
We use industry standard components unless a quantified competitive advantage can be demonstrated or when program requirements or funding dictates.	Non-supported or non-standard products put a tremendous drain on sustaining resources, driving up our costs for little to no benefit.

We plan and manage a simplified architecture and strive to reduce the complexity in today's architecture.	Complex architectures are difficult to maintain and drive up our costs.
We are standardizing on Microsoft platforms, including Windows and Office. Database Applications are required to run in a SQL Server environment unless a quantifiable business advantage exists.	Standardization allows for more coherent support, lowers the cost of ownership and allows Company to leverage its relationship with key suppliers. The Company IT Standards Process will define the standards and the process by which standards can be amended.
We select and implement long-term solutions unless a quantified competitive advantage exists.	Selecting some solutions requires trading short-term gains for long-run complexity, but this will be done with utmost consideration.
Company IT plans its infrastructure evolution. Business value and application needs will drive the plan.	We will no longer just evolve as events unfold but will set a vision architecture and plan based on where the business value is realized. We will then work to achieve the plan.
We manage and fund our technology centrally, based upon the changing needs of Company.	Technology requires centralized control and funding to achieve full leverage of costs and services.

We strive to implement the solution with the lowest Total Cost of Ownership (TCO).	Lowest TCO includes the entire life cycle of the technology, from planning through build, operation and disposal, maintenance and support, including any financing.
We will utilize the most current technology that has been demonstrated to be stable and reliable.	We will not be compelled to be on the "bleeding edge" of technology. We will, however, continually monitor the newest technology to determine when it is appropriate for us to implement it.

We plan and manage upgrades to our hardware, network and data environment using release management and configuration management.	This enables us to maintain a stable production environment through testing and validation. We will maintain our infrastructure components including desktop, laptop, network equipment and servers within their manufacturer's warranty (unless the cost of the warranty is disproportionate to the cost of the hardware). In no case will we retain devices beyond the manufacturer's End of Life designation. The Company IT Refresh Process describes the release levels we will strive to maintain. When hardware is removed from the environment but has not yet reached the end of its useful life, we will seek other individuals or organizations that can benefit from its use. When it has reached the end of its useful life, we will recycle through Company's recycling programs.

Investment Core Principles

Principle	Amplification
We purchase systems rather than custom develop our own systems unless a quantified competitive advantage can be proven.	Competitive advantage includes timing, migration cost, maintenance, support and entry barriers. Given our ERP foundation, we will seek software that interacts with the following systems, in the following order: • ERP Core Modules (Microsoft AX) • Core Applications (Microsoft RMS) • Portal Applications (SharePoint) • Software-as-a-Service Applications • Custom Develop (Using our Standard Platform)
We improve leverage by using fewer vendors, coordinating them centrally and managing them locally with significant oversight, increasing quality and control.	Quality management and control of vendors is critical to our gaining value from their relationship with Company.

We seek to develop strategic partnerships over time where they add value to our business.	Not all vendor relationships can be partnerships; strategic relationships that are good for both parties take much time and effort to develop. We will seek these benefits, but not at all costs.
We strive to do business with vendors that have a significant market presence, suitable sized staff, credentialed and qualified experience.	Small operations can sometimes appear attractive and competitive, but in the long run, they can significantly increase our risk.

Organization Core Principles

Principle	Amplification
We employ a "grow our own" staffing philosophy while obtaining short-term needs through external hiring.	We develop our staff in such a way that their careers at Company can continue to grow. We look first to our internal staff to fill any new job positions.
We retain and aggressively develop those roles that add the most VALUE to Company including: • All aspects of strategic projects • Management and leadership • Design, development, deployment, and support of our technology • Architectural design • Integration design • R&D in search of opportunities to positively impact the business • Design and development of business and IT processes and systems • Consulting to the business on process and technology issues	We will shift our skill-set and responsibilities to those areas that add the most value to the business and use the knowledge that we have about the business. We will strive to retain our employees through a culture of teamwork, fair compensation, promotion opportunities, training opportunities, credential opportunities, involvement beyond IT within the corporation, and working with the individual to understand their goals. At the same time, we acknowledge that we will not always be able to provide the career growth opportunities within Company Industries of Central Indiana.

We use contractors to accomplish tasks that: • Are better delivered due to timing, expertise or availability • Are not skills we want • Free our people for higher-value activities • Result in knowledge transfer to us	We will continue to employ contractors and consultants, as they will add flexibility to our staffing model. We will work to free our people for more valuable and interesting work.
The IT Steering Team provides direction to IT based upon business requirements. They will identify constraints, determine scheduling requirements, resolve issues escalated to them, ensure resource availability and manage project interdependencies. The IT Steering Team also serves as the overall Steering Committee for major initiatives.	Executive support and commitment is critical for spending prioritization and success of IT for projects that are cross-business initiatives.
We centralize the management of technology staff for consistency and control.	We may co-locate staff within areas of the business to ensure high levels of service and business knowledge. This may include retail locations.

We lead and manage Company IT in a way that adds maximum value to Company.	We will work hard as a professional team to ensure everyone makes smart process and technology decisions.
We partner with other Company associates to increase their knowledge of processes and technology's potential, benefits and impacts.	We will educate Company associates in the areas of technology and process to help ensure appropriate decisions are made in these areas.
We selectively outsource when it delivers superior value to Company.	We only want to do that which we can do better than others.
We continuously improve ways in which we work.	Using industry frameworks and best practices such as ITIL, CMM, COBIT, etc., will help us to constantly improve.
We strive to provide Great Customer Service	Using the Seven Steps to Great Service, we will seek ways to continually improve customer service. We will measure and report our customer's satisfaction with our services.

ABOUT THE AUTHOR

Throughout his career in business, Jeff Ton has developed and fine-tuned his leadership skills to become a business focused leader who drives results. He brings a strategic view of business and identifies innovative approaches to achieve business objectives by leveraging technology where and when appropriate. Adept at building and leading teams, both in-line and cross-organizational, he has been a catalyst for change across the businesses he has served.

Ton is an executive with InterVision, an information technology managed service provider. He is responsible for driving the company's product and service vision and strategy. Jeff focuses on the evolving IT landscape and the changing needs of the company's clients, and, together with the InterVision team, ensures their products and services meet their client's needs and drives value within their organizations now and in the future.

Prior to joining InterVision, Jeff spent 5 years at Goodwill Industries of Central Indiana where he led the development and implementation of the enterprise-wide information technology portfolio, including applications, infrastructure, security and telecommunications across the Goodwill business units. Taking a cloud-first approach, IT transformed into a partner with the business units, providing significant value throughout the organization. He has owned his own management consulting firm and was the CIO for Lauth Property Group. Prior to Lauth, Ton spent 14 years in various technology roles with Technicolor (Thomson Multimedia (RCA)).

He serves on various boards and advisory councils including: Hoosier Environmental Council board of directors, Indiana Network of Knowledge Governance Committee, Connected World Magazine Board of Advisors, CIT Industrial Advisory Board (IUPUI), SAVI Technical Advisory Committee (The Polis Center) and the Mud Creek Conservancy.

Jeff also spends time as a keynote speaker, blogger and writer on a wide variety of topics, including leadership, employee development, technology, and business operations. Away from work, he and his wife enjoy family, canoeing, gardening, history and travel.

Connect with Jeff on LinkedIn at
www.linkedin.com/in/jeffton

and follow him on Twitter:
https://twitter.com/jtonindy.

SPEAKING

IS YOUR ORGANIZATION IN NEED OF A SPEAKER? Jeff is available for keynote speeches, breakout sessions, or workshops.

Over the past 30 years as a, veteran in business, Jeff has developed a casual, entertaining, and educational style of creating a dialogue with groups from 5 to 1,000 to help inspire, motivate, and guide. He has combined his experiences in a variety of industries with his passions for leadership, history, music, the outdoors and the environment, and the lessons learned along the way. This combination in addition to his own role models, his parents—his mother was an author and speaker, his father was a preacher—have created, in him, a unique style of leadership and presenting.

To learn more visit: https://riversofthought.net/public-speaking